Joseph H. William
2/19/2013

Who Do You See in the Mirror?

Change irresponsible behavior in the workplace to responsible behavior.

Joseph A. Williams, Ph.D.

Editor: Bree K. James
Designer: Sue Campbell
Photographer: Randy Carr

Cataloging in Publication data available.

ISBN-10: 0-615-26855-2
ISBN-13: 978-0-615-26855-2

Published by Common Sense Management Strategies (CSMS)
Henderson, Nevada 89011
Phone 702-567-3051 • Fax: 702-567-3054
http://www.drjawcsms.com

Printed in the United States of America

This book is dedicated to my two daughters, April and Eva. My greatest hope is that they can live in a world with a responsible behavioral environment, and pass the culture of responsibility on to future generations. May they use this style of behavior to enhance their journeys.

In memory of my parents Ada and Bob, and my brothers Bobby, Rudy, Donald, Cliff, and Malcolm.

CONTENTS

Acknowledgments

My wife Janett Rice, who inspired me to write this book, is also a published author and understands the writing process. With this in mind I thank her most of all for her never-ending patience as this book was being written. I also thank her for the creative ideas she contributed and her tough but oh, so necessary editing skills. Janett spent copious hours reading and critiquing my writing with minimal complaint. For this I remain forever grateful.

Special recognition also goes to Bree K. James for her outstanding contributions that made this book possible. Bree took dry technical information and brought it to life. She is an exceptional story-telling editor, and this book would not have been the same without her experience and coaching.

Meredith McGhan, Linda O'Connor and O'Brien Young all added significant expertise and their own unique individual touches during the editing process. Other editing contributors include Leslie Hoffman and Suzanne Bergfalk, Ph.D.

In the process of formulating the Human Cable System™ (HCS), it was necessary for me to accurately apply theories of educational psychology and organizational behavior during early human development. Associate Professor Lisa D. Bendixen, Ph.D. in the Department of Educational Psychology, and Professor Alder Stoney Ph.D. in the College of Business Management, University of Nevada–Las Vegas, deserve special recognition for sharing their expertise in those areas with me.

No manuscript can be successfully written without the open and frank criticism of its readers. Special thanks go to Dorothy Rasmussen, Ph.D. and Patty Brown, two readers who read the manuscript in its infancy and made comments that helped it grow into a mature adult. Thanks also go to Billee Platt and Barbara Jones for their contributions.

I am grateful to Candie and Rayneen Cervantes for sharing real life experiences when I was desperately seeking interesting examples of behavioral situations. Thanks go to Dorothy Rasmussen and her son Daniel for their story sharing contributions. There were also numerous employees, interviewed at international airport during my travels, that shared their experiences relating to a variety of behavioral issues.

Many companies and organizations participated in the gathering of research data. These companies include: Costco, Office Max, University of Phoenix, Warm Springs Dental, Henderson Writers Group, Avista Eye Center East, Transport Workers Union of America, AFL-CIO, and St. James United Methodist Church, Kansas City, Missouri. Their cooperation was especially appreciated.

Introduction

WHO DO YOU SEE IN THE MIRROR? IS A STORY ABOUT DEALING FACE-TO-FACE with human behavior. Everyone in the world—an estimated 6.8 billion of us—exhibits or is influenced by two types of behavior: responsible or irresponsible. **Behavior is everything that humans do,** linking their actions and inactions in response to the stimulation of their environment. Behavior has no age, sex, or national origin boundaries. Responsible or irresponsible human behavior penetrates all social structures: businesses, governments, political institutions, churches, schools, and communities. And, human behavior also enters into every personal interaction in life. Behavior accounts for all of the problems the world is facing today and their future solutions.

People's actions and inactions have a ripple effect, either negative or positive, in establishing our global behavioral environment. Many of the behaviors we see in today's society suggest we are shifting toward a culture of irresponsibility. A culture of irresponsibility consists of people who are out of control and display carelessness, immaturity, dishonesty, corruption, and are in a state of denial. It also includes people who lack courage and good work ethics, and regularly blame others for their own actions. The trend toward irresponsibility is a greater threat to the world's security than the proliferation of nuclear weapons or guns. Weapons themselves, being inanimate objects, do not kill. Killing occurs as a result of human action.

Economists have estimated that the total world's labor force in the current global economy is approximately 1.5 billion people. However, with China, India, and Russia entering the labor market, an additional 1.5 billion people will be competing in the global economy. This brings the total world labor force to about 3 billion people, about 50 percent of the world population, that are being influenced by the ripple effect of responsible and irresponsible behavior.

Individual human behavior connects the global behavioral environment. The labor force will mirror the behavior of its culture. If society displays irresponsible behavior, creating a culture of irresponsibility, the workplace behavioral environment will suffer the same shift toward irresponsibility.

Irresponsibility is a serious threat to the success of the workplace behavioral environment. An enterprise is the non-living organ of the business organization, and, as such, it cannot decide, act, or behave by itself. Therefore, the enterprise has no effective existence by itself. A business succeeds or fails according to the responsible or irresponsible behavior of its personnel, both management and non-management, the living organ of the organization. All personnel must work together, executing responsible actions, to achieve the goals of the enterprise. Employees must be held accountable for the successes and failures of a business.

The same can be said of our government's workplaces. Government, as an organized structure, is a non-living element, which cannot function without the actions of the members of the Congressional and Executive branches working together responsibly for the causes of the voters who elected them, and with the Judicial branch to ensure the rights guaranteed by our Constitution. If these bodies behave irresponsibly, the voters' wishes are disregarded, and the global culture of irresponsibility is strengthened.

Human behavior is the source of most problems and their ultimate solutions in today's global society. The recession America and other nations are experiencing should remind us just how much human behavior is connected. America's economic crisis has had a domino effect on the economies of other nations. Despite the cultural differences, all people in the world share the instinct to survive, and the desire to be respected and achieve self-actualization.

There exists today a sense of urgency to seek common sense solutions for a sustainable change. This requires responsible action on a global level. What has gotten in the way of this? Some say the world is too complex, but perhaps it is because the mindset of denial, lack of courage and fear of self-incrimination reflects back at people when looking into the mirror.

Who Do You See in the Mirror? addresses the larger issue of responsible and irresponsible behavior, with its primary focus targeting workplace behavior. It also looks at related causes and effects of behavior that often stem from the developmental structure established in childhood. This book will help anyone working with others to deal directly with the question: What do you see in the mirror: responsible or irresponsible behavior in the workplace?

The purpose of *Who Do You See in the Mirror?* is to help employers and employees identify and understand workplace-related actions and inactions that may result from their own unique behavioral backgrounds. The process involves using a simple innovative concept called the Human CABLE System (HCS), and the Twelve Common Sense Principles for Responsible Behavior to create a more responsible workplace culture.

The HCS, used as a self-help tool, offers a clear way to be part of a responsible workplace environment. Using HCS can help answer the question, "Who Do You See in the Mirror?" The consequences of your attitude, behavior, learning, and environment are much closer to each other than people realize.

Although there has been much scholarly enterprise involved in gathering and creating the material for this book, Dr. Williams is also "just Joe" to the many workers he met and worked beside. Stepping outside his experiences in the academic and corporate world—where he accomplished 30 years of successful employment—Dr. Williams decided to "walk his talk" and took a job as a baggage handler at a major airport.

The following stories are inspired by the many surveys, interviews and conversations Dr. Williams conducted with working people.

The participants in the weekly coffee shop meetings in the book are composites of the actual people and events. The "character" of Joe is both a realistic portrayal of Dr. Williams, and a reflection of the feedback he received from the people who became the coffee shop group.

CHAPTER ONE

Saving the World,
One Coffee Shop at a Time

Begin with yourself to see change in the world!
For a shift toward a society of more responsible behavior,
who do you see in the mirror?

E VERY MONDAY AFTER WORK, JOE STOPPED AT A LOCAL COFFEE SHOP TO unwind before going home for the evening. This coffee shop, near the business district and a major airport, had become a favorite hangout for many of the working class people employed nearby. Its atmosphere provided them with a safe haven in which to escape their job responsibilities and relax after a stressful day in the workplace.

It had become a tradition for a regular group of workers to stop by the coffee shop on Monday evenings to spend about an hour before going home for the evening. Since this was a weekly gathering, the coffee shop servers became familiar with the faces, names, and favorite drinks of the regulars. When they arrived at the shop, each would be greeted with a friendly smile, a bit of small talk, and his or her favorite beverage.

There was camaraderie among the regulars, and they usually started the evening inquiring about each other's work day and families, and then often proceeded to discuss a national or international issue that they felt affected them at work. They shared a common interest in discussing new ideas to resolve their work issues. As Barbara, a bookkeeper at one of the larger food suppliers at the airport, said one evening, "Did you know that more than 50 percent of working people's waking hours are spent on the job? It just makes sense that if our lives were better at work, the world would be better, too."

One of the concerns the regulars shared is what they saw as a trend toward irresponsible behavior at their respective businesses. The indictments of corporate securities fraud and falsification of business records that resulted in the convictions of several top executives, investigations of wrongdoing by government officials and employees, and thousands of people dealing with cancellations of airline flights due to neglected inspections were constantly in the news and gave the group members grist for the mill of their discontent. Barbara brought up a report by the FBI she had seen on the Internet, telling her companions, "It said corruption had increased 30 percent over the past year."

Edward, who had been working for over 15 years as a mechanic at a large garage, shook his head and said, "It seems that no one these days wants to take responsibility for what they do or don't do. Those convicted executives blew off their responsibility for the consequences of their actions! They're always ready to say, 'Oh, no, it wasn't me, I had nothing to do with it' ... and point the finger at somebody else—and usually somebody who is lower than they are on the totem pole."

Brian, a hotel desk clerk, responded to Edward, "Seriously, it's not just a problem of these big-time execs in the news. It's my manager and then his manager and then his manager and on and on. This lack of responsibility thing goes all up and down the ladder."

"Right you are," Edward agreed. "And it's got this ripple effect that makes where you work a negative scene." The regulars felt this irresponsibility issue was out of control and needed to be fixed, and the coffee shop gatherings were the perfect setting to come up with ideas to resolve the problem.

A server who had been avidly listening to the discussion remarked, "You'd be surprised how many problems are resolved in coffee shops just like this one."

Joe overheard this discussion and it really caught his attention—what the coffee shop patrons were talking about was precisely his area of interest, and he saw a great opportunity to help the group with his skills and further his own study of the subject at the same time. It was not too long before Joe became one of the regular patrons, and over time, it became clear to his companions that Joe had some ideas that could improve life at work for them all. The Monday evening gathering at the coffee shop turned into a sort of casual seminar. People came to learn about Joe's concepts about behavior on the job being the root cause of the positive or negative cultures in their workplaces.

Joe knew he was quite different from the group of regulars. He had 30 years of management experience after working for two Fortune 500 companies, and because he wanted to remain mentally active, he went back to graduate school after retiring.

"You're a good example that an old dog can learn new tricks!" Brian said when he heard that Joe completed his doctorate in Applied Management and Decision Science at 65-years-old. "Now tell me what all that means, and why the heck you're working as a baggage handler, and I'll buy your coffee tonight."

Joe explained to Brian and the rest of the group that when he was an executive in the corporate world, he often wondered why today's businesses didn't consider it more important to focus on the human behavioral aspect of the organization. "After all," he told them, "behavior is the common element shared by all issues." Believing that a person's actions and inactions are the most critical factors in determining an individual's moral fiber and the success or failure of an organization, Joe developed his own innovative ideas.

"It's simply that some people act responsibly when responding to situations and others act irresponsibly," he said. "But this is a mighty thing, because it goes beyond the workplace. I'm hoping I can help you figure out how to make some things in your work lives better, and I'm hoping you can help me answer two questions I've been working on for quite a while: What is the connection between behavior in the workplace and an individual's early childhood environment? And how can people's irresponsible behavior be corrected?"

Joe was an efficient facilitator at the Monday evening get togethers, and was able to help the group define and frame an issue before focusing on a solution. The others encouraged Joe to lead most discussions, both because he was considered the common sense behavioral expert, and because his enthusiasm for the topic of the day was contagious. Occasionally, the regulars would ask him questions or offer their points of view to spur the discussion forward.

Sometimes Joe would present the group with an issue, and then invite them to dream of the best possible outcome." I believe this," he told them, "if you can dream a positive outcome you can achieve it." He told the group stories about people's behavior in real life situations, sometimes using metaphorical characters and concepts, but always bringing in two basic behavioral principles that were central to his philosophy:

1. **Responsible or irresponsible behavior is the sole source of a human being's acts. These acts are creations and activities that result in success or failure.**

2. **To resolve a problem or improve a situation and achieve real sustainable progress the root cause of the issue's success or failure must be dealt with directly as well as the related cause and effects connected with the problem.**

Joe found the metaphor of looking at oneself in the mirror helped people see themselves objectively—something that he knew was necessary in order to make sustainable behavioral changes. One day Greg, an airport van driver, asked Joe, "Why do you use mirrors in most of your explanations and discussions?" Joe replied, "The mirror is a tool to unmask people's self-denial. It helps us deal directly with the root cause of many issues, and helps me find real sustainable solutions to those issues." He then proceeded to share the story of how the mirror became such an important part of his story analogies.

"When I was a young boy, my mother frequently had to remind me that if I really wanted to help make the world a better place in

18

which to live, I would have to 'begin with the person I saw in the mirror.' Her words stayed with me to this day, although, the phrase took on different meanings as I matured in life. At the age of twelve I understood her words to mean that I should take a good look at my own appearance before I looked at other people's appearances, and looking in the mirror became a daily routine.

"I became obsessed with my appearance. Thinking about this, I realized that looking in the mirror was the only way a person could come face to face with the truth of him or herself. The mirror has always symbolized honesty because the mirror's image never lies. It conveys the same absolute truth, as does the human body. It tells the truth of how we look before we comb and brush our hair, apply make-up, or dress for the day.

"My thought process at age twelve could not get past the physical appearance of the image reflecting back. People today are even more obsessed with the way they look than I was then. So much so, they are willing to spend billions of dollars on plastic surgery, altering their appearances by giving themselves a physical makeover instead of altering their behavior for an internal character makeover.

"As I got older I realized my mother reminded me about looking at myself in the mirror when I acted irresponsibly, not when she was trying to say something about how I looked. She was telling me not to let the physical attributes reflecting from the mirror blind me from seeing the attributes of my character. I came to understand that this is the true center of beauty: moral character. A person's physical appearance is only skin-deep and fades with age, whereas, a person's character will never fade, and will last well past physical life on this earth.

"Making this critical behavioral connection helped me to get past the physical appearance mentality. I began to think on a much broader horizon. The reflection of the mirror image mimics all of an individual's actions. In this situation, I am in complete control of the actions of the reflected image. I cannot blame others or deny the fact that I am responsible and accountable for the acts of my reflected image. However, being faced with the reality of my physical attributes, I still had a tendency to blame my parents for my dissatisfaction about the way my eyes, hair, nose, and lips looked.

"After all, I did not bring myself into the world; it was an action taken by my parents. While I played the blame game, I blamed my pants for being too tight to fit me comfortably anymore. It was either the fault of the pants manufacturer or the cooks of the food I ate. I did not accept the fact that I chose to eat too much. Blaming others for such tangible things such as the pants or food, was my way of feeling better about myself by seeking pleasure and avoiding emotional pain."

"So, what you are saying," Edward commented, "is that consciously or unconsciously, people behave by seeking pleasure and avoiding pain, right?"

"Right," Joe responded. "It's a built-in survival instinct that comes with being human. Pain is suffering resulting from physical, mental, or emotional distress. Pleasure is the result of being satisfied. Pain and pleasure can vary from person to person. What one person sees as pain, another person sees as pleasure, or vice-versa depending on the circumstances."

"I just know you're going to tell us how this relates to work," said Brian, drawing a chuckle from the others, a group that had settled into a dozen or so people who made a commitment to the Monday night meetings.

Joe nodded, smiling. "Why, yes, I am, Brian, and here's what it is. In the workplace environment, workers will typically seek tasks they enjoy doing and avoid stressful tasks, even though they know the job requires the completion of the stressful tasks. So, employers attempt to match the tasks with workers who enjoy performing them, because this increases morale and productivity.

"These same workers, who enjoy performing their tasks, are also more willing to be responsible and accountable for the outcome. Matching a worker's incentive to perform a task to the task being asked of them is a win-win situation for both the employer and employee, as long as it does not stifle flexibility of the workforce.

"Workers, who attempt to avoid tasks that are stressful while still having to perform them, have a tendency to blame the procedure or others for the outcome if it is not successful."

Ellen, a security guard and single mother of two, asked, "How did the workplace reach a point of being almost immune to people accepting responsibility for their own actions and inactions?"

"That's a good question for next Monday's gathering," Joe replied, suggesting three discussion topics for the following week. "First, let's define the issue of responsible versus irresponsible behavior in the workplace so we're all on the same page. Second, we can try to determine how big this issue is, and third, I'll share some things I know about the history of how the workplace got to where not taking responsibility for one's own behavior became so fashionable in today's environment.

"This will be a bit like looking at the issue in a rear view mirror," Joe concluded. "We can look at where the behavior of the workplace environment has been, so we can see where behavior in the workplace environment is going—always a good idea before changing lanes."

Chapter Two

Common Sense Principles, A Standard Workplace Guide

THE REGULARS BEGAN GATHERING AT THE COFFEE SHOP AROUND FIVE P.M. Joe began the discussion. "Picking up where we ended last Monday's discussion, here are some examples of employee actions that describe responsible versus irresponsible behavior in the workplace. We all need to have a clear, comprehensive definition of the problem behavior before we attempt to fix it.

"First, here are some examples of responsible behavior characteristics in the workplace." He handed a small stack of papers to Brian and asked him to pass them around. "I think it's always easier to have a list like this in front of you, so you don't have to be trying to write it down on your napkin," he said, smiling, and got a few laughs from the people who had been about to do just that. Joe read the list:

1. **Responsible employees don't need guidance or supervision. They can be trusted to do their work correctly and independently.**

2. **They usually perform tasks with integrity, putting forth their best effort.**

3. **Proactively, they take into account the consequences of their actions before reacting to a situation. They openly display the courage to take responsibility for their actions without blaming others.**

4. **They also have the courage to do the right thing when confronted with difficulties that challenge their character.**

5. **They consistently report to work on time. They treat themselves and other employees with respect and dignity.**

"These principles of responsible behavior are plain, common sense actions," Joe said. "Later in this discussion, we can use these characteristics to develop some common sense principles of responsible behavior that can be used as a standard guide in the workplace and throughout life.

"A good role model for responsible behavior is the president and CEO of Japan Airlines, Haruka Nishimatsu," Joe continued. "The CEO goes to work on a public bus, not private corporate jets. He also cut his salary to about $90,000 a year when he proposed cutting the salary of his employees. He even removed the walls from his office so he'd be more accessible and exemplify a true open door policy to his employees."

Ellen commented, "What you just described sounds like a good work ethic and just what today's workforce seems to be moving away from."

"Yeah, that certainly is a good example of a responsible executive," Edward responded, "but when I told my sister what we were talking about, she e-mailed me this article about Merrill Lynch CEO John Thain, who spent $1 million decorating his office."

"Yes," Joe said, "I'm afraid there are more examples of this kind of irresponsible corporate behavior. Did you know that Citigroup executives had planned to purchase a new $50 million corporate jet at the same time they were receiving billions of dollars in tax payer bailouts?"

These examples touched a lot of nerves in the room. Head shaking and muttering ensued. But Joe thought it was important to get the group activated enough to truly want to help make change happen, so he risked continuing in this vein. "Likewise," he said, his serious tone capturing the restless group's attention, "regardless of the losses in investor retirement accounts and the huge taxpayer money bailout, Wall Street gave out more than $18 billion in bonuses in 2008."

"Well, that's what President Obama was talking about!" Brian exclaimed. "I heard him blasting these selfish executives for asking taxpayers to give them all this money, and how we're in a bind because if we don't provide help, the whole system could come down on top of our heads."

"I heard that, too," Barbara added. "He said that it's the height of irresponsibility and shameful. And then right after the even bigger bailout from the government—over $8 billion, right?—executives at the same companies that were getting this money took huge bonuses! The President was really angry about that, too."

"Indeed," said Joe. "I'm afraid we could cite many more examples of irresponsibility by corporate leaders. Let's turn those sheets over now and look at my list of the behaviors exhibited by irresponsible employees." And with the soft flutter of papers being flipped around the room, Joe read this list to the group:

1. **They often go against the rules, are driven by impulse, and seldom consider the consequences of their actions.**

2. **They rarely take responsibility for their actions or inactions.**

3. **They cannot be trusted to do their work independently, or with integrity. A fraud-based attitude tends to drive their response to the behavioral environment.**

4. **Rarely do they put forth their best effort.**

5. **Blaming others for their own actions becomes a pattern in their behavior. They often abdicate their responsibility and then look for a scapegoat to cover their inaction.**

6. **They have little respect for themselves, others, or for the company's property.**

7. They consistently report to work late, using excuses for their lateness.

8. When working on a team, they do not contribute their fair share of the work and spend a lot of time thinking of ways to get out of doing their work.

"I agree that irresponsible employees have an attitude toward fraud," said Barbara. "This is going back a bit, but for me it was one of my first times of being aware of how badly people can behave in a company. Maybe it kind of set the stage for the more recent outrages. I'm talking about Enron, you know, the energy company? It was found to be guilty of one of the biggest swindles in U.S. history. Enron once employed about 21,000 people, and after the financial fraud scandal, it employed only about 6,000."

Brian interrupted, "Barbara, we can always count on you to know the numbers!"

Barbara blushed a little at the compliment and continued, "It was shocking to learn that Enron, once the world's leading electricity, natural gas, pulp and paper, and communications company, committed such an irresponsible act. Enron's top executives once claimed as much as $111 billion in revenue. But, it was later revealed that its financial picture was deliberately and creatively *planned accounting fraud.*"

"How could anyone forget this display of irresponsible behavior," added Ellen. "It was not the kind of record those top executives were shooting for, but Enron is now known as the largest corporate failure in world history due to criminal acts."

"That's for sure," Barbara responded. "It was the largest and most complex bankruptcy case in U.S. history. It's estimated that Enron's losses exceeded $68 billion."

"Enron's fraud scandal caused the end of the Arthur Andersen accounting firm," said Edward, "which had a ripple effect on the whole business world. Their irresponsible behavior cast a cloud of suspicion over other corporations and accounting firms serving the public—how can we trust any of them?"

"What I read was that the Enron financial scandal happened when CEOs lied about their financial holdings," Ellen said. "The CEOs mislead investors and employees, and then denied responsibility for the result. The whole Wall Street mess proves that situations like Enron's are increasing, and some people seem to think that irresponsible acts such as these are just the tip of the iceberg. In today's workplaces, there is a lot of suspicion about just how widespread these corporate scandals are."

"Well," chimed in Greg, "scandals aren't confined to the private businesses. Let's not forget about irresponsible behavior in government, when local, state, and federal officials are involved in taking bribes for favors given to special-interest groups."

Joe nodded agreement and said, "The disjointed responses by local, state, and federal governments to the damage caused by Hurricanes Katrina and Rita are also examples of abdicating responsibility. There were allegations surrounding improper distribution of federal dollars to people affected by the hurricanes. And at the same time others not affected by the hurricanes received government money. This is a situation where some people took advantage of the opportunity to commit fraud."

"And what about the officials in the Pentagon who misused billions of dollars?" Ellen asked. "They spent all this money on personal luxuries instead of directing it to the war efforts. It's unconscionable that such a scandalous act was perpetrated while our soldiers were losing their lives in the Iraq war."

"So true," Edward said. "Money is so often the main incentive for negative behavior whether it's a public, private, or government workplace. I hear this expression often in break room conversations at work when these sorts of scandals surface. People say 'money is the root of all evil,' and it seems that if money is involved as a temptation, some people are easily seduced into committing acts of corruption."

When Edward mentioned the saying "money is the root of all evil," Joe decided this was a good time to clarify the difference between the motivations caused by living versus non-living things.

"We pointed out in a previous discussion the behavioral differences that might shed some light on the saying 'money is the root of all evil.' To reiterate, an inanimate entity such as an enterprise is a non-living organ of a business and is incapable of behaving or taking action without employees. The employees form the living organ. Other examples include the various branches of our government that are non-living organs and are incapable of behaving without the actions of the members.

"Likewise," Joe continued, "the saying 'money is the root of all evil,' is an inaccurate statement, because money is a non-living material possession that is used as a medium of exchange. Money cannot act by casting an evil spell over a person that causes the person to commit fraud—just as an enterprise cannot run itself without the actions of its employees. The lesson here is that only people, the living forms of life, can commit fraud.

"The saying 'money is the root of all evil' originated in the New Testament. To be exact the quote is 'For the love of money is the root of all evil,' Timothy, 6:10. That saying has been misquoted for thousands of years and is still being misquoted today."

"Really!" said Brian. "I didn't realize it came from the Bible."

"I would guess that a lot of people today don't know the origin if they're not church goers" said Barbara, "but this is how people's actions influence what Joe calls the 'behavioral environment.' One person misquotes the saying. When others hear it, they don't question the correctness of the saying, and the misquoted saying is repeated enough times until it becomes fashionable. The incorrect saying becomes the one everyone knows."

"Yeah," added Brian. "It's like the game of Gossip we used to play as kids, whispering something from person to person and hearing how it came out at the end of the line. The last kid said out loud what he or she thought they'd heard and the result was often very funny because it had nothing at all to do with the original statement. It could start out as, 'James and Melanie went to the store and bought six oranges,' and end up as 'Games on linoleum get stoves sent abroad with orangutans!'"

Joe laughed along with the others and then said, "Exactly. Yet the context of the two sayings is completely different. In the phrase 'For the love of money is the root of all evil,' love is a feeling expressed toward a person, an object, money, a job, food, etc. Money is a measure of status in life. But more important, a person's character is often measured by his or her response to money. People are often confused between *money*, *status*, and the resulting *behavior*.

"They amass money to achieve status rather than to pay the bills. These are two different motivations. Amassing money to pay bills is a reaction based on survival. How much money a person has accumulated is one way to measure wealth. So, is it not fair to blame all evil on money, or even any evil at all, really, since money is a non-living substance? Money is incapable of behaving."

"So, if money is not the root of all evil, what is?" asked Edward.

"Before I answer your questions, I would like to explain a common cause of evil acts displayed by people," responded Joe. "It's jealousy.

"Jealousy is a common cause of evil and can take many different forms in the workplace. It is often connected to money. For example, an employee can become jealous of another employee because he or she makes more money. The most common evil acts displayed among employees in the workplace center around inequitable work assignments and mistreatment that may not have anything to do with money. But, those things have everything to do with the employees' irresponsible behavior. Situations such as sexual and racial harassment, verbal abuse, and discrimination come to mind.

"By the same token," continued Joe, "amassing money for the love of money can be evil or good whether you are an entrepreneur or employee. As an example, suppose an entrepreneur loves to accumulate money for the purpose of giving it away to make the world a better place. Say, the entrepreneur gives it away to help find a cure for cancer, diabetes, or heart disease, and donates money to help educate less fortunate people so those people can help themselves and pass it on to others in the world. These are examples where money is used for doing good things, not evil.

Obviously, there is status gained for giving money away for a good cause, and some of the richest people in the world have gained such status of being generous with their wealth. Nonetheless, you can't say that having money has caused these philanthropists to act in an evil way.

28

"The other side of this debate is a selfish entrepreneur or employee who loves money to the degree of being obsessed with it. This entrepreneur's or employee's behavior is a more accurate description of what the phrase 'for the love of money is the root of all evil' addresses. But even in this scenario, money, being a non-living substance, cannot be blamed for people's obsessive and selfish behavior regarding it.

"So, to answer the question you asked earlier, people's behavior—regarding money and everything else in life—is actually the root of all evil. It's even more accurate to say that human behavior—action or inaction—is the root cause of evil or good. There are many examples where money is blamed for irresponsible behaviors. And these instances are common occurrences costing organizations billions of dollars in lack of productivity."

"I can think of a bunch of things people have done at work that I'd call irresponsible," said Ellen, "but then I imagine all sorts of reasons they might have for doing what they've done. Joe, I'll bet you have some good stories that might help us understand how to figure out when to take something seriously, right?"

"Indeed I do," replied Joe, "And that sounds like a good place to start next time—this has been a long and meaningful discussion and we all have a lot to think about, so how about we begin with some story telling next week?"

The group agreed and, as promised, the following Monday, Joe shared a typical story about the absenteeism that runs rampant throughout most workplace environments. When everyone was settled, he began.

"A supervisor asked one of his subordinates to come to his office for a performance review.

"'I reviewed your records,' the supervisor said, 'and I noticed that your absentee rate is 10 percent. Monday is the day that you call in sick more often than any other day. Could you help me understand? Why Monday?'

"'Just between you and me, the work is boring,' the employee said. 'If I don't use up my sick days, company policy doesn't let me carry them over to next year or get paid for them. If I don't use them, I lose them, so I take a lot of nice long weekends."

"The supervisor thought to himself, *'Employees with a sense of entitlement are ruining this company! They're the reason I always have to be the bad guy.'*

"'But sick days are not vacation days. You're only supposed to use sick days if you get sick,' said the supervisor."

"'Really?' The employee seemed befuddled. 'But that just doesn't seem fair!'"

"I imagine we all can relate to that story," said Joe, and agreement rolled around the room.

Susan, a regular with the group who rarely spoke up, was clearly brought to attention by this topic. "I work in one of the gift stores at the airport," she said.

"Employees who regularly report to work late also create problems. Being late is almost as bad as being absent for the day in terms of the inconvenience it can cause. In retail businesses, employees who are responsible for opening the store at a specific time will miss out on sales if they don't open the store on time. And I can't tell you how many times I've had to wait for the person taking over my place at the cash register when they're late for their shift. I try to continue to give good service to the customers, but it's hard when I'm tired and starting to get annoyed that I'm still working and not getting paid for it! I have a family to get home to—well, except on Mondays when I come here," she said, her frown of frustration softening into a smile.

"The airline industry is another situation where being on time is really important," said Greg. "I mean, the airline's goal is to get travelers, bags, cargos, and mail from location A to location B safely and on time. If a worker with some of the responsibility for achieving that goal, like myself and the other van drivers, are late or absent, there's a whole chain of other services that are affected, and complaints end up on the person's record. Getting your co-workers and everybody up the line in a bind sure isn't a way to advance your career."

"What really drives me nuts," chimed in Brian, "are the lame excuses people give for being late: 'I forgot to set my alarm clock,' 'I got stuck in traffic,' or 'I forgot to change my clock to daylight savings time.' I was working night shift at the hotel one time, when the person relieving me was almost two hours late—I was falling asleep at the desk! You know what she said when she finally showed up? Her hair dryer caught fire and she had to go to the store to buy another one and then go back home and do her hair! I'll tell you, the excuse about that girl's hair was nothing you'd put on an employee evaluation as superlative employee performance!" Brian flicked his own hair off his forehead as if those strands were the center of his universe.

After the laughter over Brian's spontaneous imitation died down, Barbara brought a serious tone back to the room. "On the other hand," she said, "bosses and supervisors who fail to deal with employees being late or absent too often can also contribute to establishing the environment of irresponsibility Joe's been talking about."

"I agree," said Edward. "But what are responsible upper management people supposed to do? When bosses try to fix the problem of middle and lower management not following the absentee and lateness rules with the people they're supervising, they need to be consistent and to apply those rules all the time to everybody working at their company—including the top execs and themselves. And they should really back up their action with more than just some memo going into a file."

"Exactly," said Joe. "Management personnel must practice what they preach. Leadership starts with management from the top. It's my experience that a strategy of changing irresponsible behavior into responsible actions starting from the bottom up has little or no chance of sustaining the change. So, a company's management personnel must be willing to model punctuality in order to get that sustainable change. Ideally, the modeled behavior will end the tardiness. Otherwise, attempts to fix the problem will be short lived and efforts wasted."

"That's an interesting point you made, Joe, on leadership starting from the top," added Susan. "I think a situation that happened at the gift shop is a good example of ineffective action taken by a manager. One of the supervisors at the store, who had his own problem with tardiness, was allowed to counsel the people working under him for the same problem. It was pretty awkward for him, because the people he was getting after knew he was late more than they were! So, if I'm getting what Joe is saying correctly, that manager was being irresponsible to reprimand the late workers when he was doing the same thing."

"Right, thanks, Susan," Joe responded. "The manager's behavior and words sent out a mixed and thus irresponsible message to the workforce "Namely, *do as I say, not as I do.* In other words, the tardiness policy in that situation only applied to non-management personnel. This approach has never worked in providing guidelines that change the behavior of employees. The approach of telling employees to comply with a rule that the employers are not willing to comply with themselves is not realistic, and it's hypocritical. The employer who is attempting to apply the rule is in a state of denial about his or her own behavior. Employers must be willing to look in the mirror and start with the image they see reflecting back before they can begin enforcing behavioral polices for their employees.

"This method relates to much of early childhood development. The *do what I say, not what I do* approach has been passed down from generation to generation," Joe continued "This approach did not work during past generations, at least not in the long run, and does not work today either in the workplace or in life. Although the method has been around for years, it has never influenced people to make long-lasting changes in their behavior. Why would you want to infantilize employees anyway? Treating employees like children sets up a false power structure, as well as one that most people will resist.

"This approach seemed to work in past generations simply because of the respect some children had for their parents. This kind of respect was demonstrated in what I'd call surface level reactions. The children felt ambivalent about their parents doing the very thing that they told them not to do. Even parents often doubted that this approach would work. Parental actions were based on hoping that it would work. Most of the children who complied with that rule of *do what I say and not what I do* were eager to become adults so they could do the very things their parents told them not to do. Correctly, children viewed their parents as hypocritical. Some children voiced their disapproval, others remained silent, and still others rebelled.

"When children questioned their parents, the parents tried to justify their position by saying, 'I want you to grow up to be better than me.' Some parents claimed, 'I don't want you to make the same mistakes I made.' But parents kept making the same mistakes, and there was no real learning taking place in the next generation. For children, observing their parents making the same mistakes had more influence on the children's future behavior than their parents' verbal message.

"To put it simply, applying the theory that 'actions speak louder than words,' in today's behavioral society, could be revised to 'responsible actions speak louder than words. *Do what I say, not what I do* should also not be applied as a strategy in the workplace to guide the actions of employees. This is irresponsible behavior. Setting an example of responsible behavior is the only effective strategy to use as a guide in the workplace and in everyday life."

Joe straightened up in his chair and a worried crease appeared on his forehead. His tone was quieter when he continued, and the group unconsciously leaned in toward him. "A truly dreadful example of a workplace environment that is totally out of control is when violence occurs in that environment," he said after a thoughtful pause. "Like when employees are involved in a physical fight or shooting at work. Unfortunately, it happens more often than we realize. The local media will often report a shooting incident, but fights among employees that turn physical will probably not make the news. We all know about shootings that have occurred at post offices and schools. However, violent shootings have also happened in the private business sector." The room remained quiet as each person present recalled some of those terrible events.

Joe knew this topic was disturbing to them all, but it was important to continue, so he cleared his throat to let his listeners know there was more and went on. "When violent behavior occurs in the workplace," he said, "it is a sign that the behavioral system of the organization is broken and has been for some time. Build-up for this type of overt behavioral situation did not happen overnight. Chances are that both employer and employees have ignored the warning signs of fights or violence. The irresponsible behavior of inaction has allowed the potential for violence to fester. The bottom line is that it has not been handled with a sense of urgency by either the employer or the employees, and the outcome is violent."

"Our company has a policy for addressing on-the-job violence," Edward said. "The policy clearly states that any employee involved in a violent act, like a fist fight, will be terminated immediately. Yet, two employees were involved in a heated argument, and when tempers flared, their argument became a fistfight. The boss gave them a three-day suspension without pay. After that, they were both allowed to come back to work. Everybody working at the garage sure got the message that the organization's words don't match their actions. I think this is a case where the actions of both the boss and the employees contributed to that shift toward workplace irresponsibility we've been talking about."

"These real life stories about actions or inactions seem to show that irresponsible behavior is becoming more common in the workplace," Joe concluded. "In framing this issue, it brings us to the second topic. How big is the responsible versus irresponsible behavior problem in today's society?"

Joe looked at his watch. It was time to bring the gathering to a close. "Why don't we start with that next Monday? As each of you go through your workweek, think about the scope of the problem. Also, reflect about the history of how the workplace got to the point where irresponsibility has become so fashionable. I believe the history will offer some interesting insights."

CHAPTER THREE

Scope and History,
Common Sense Choices

THE NEXT WEEK, JOE WAS HAPPY TO SEE THAT SUSAN HAD TAKEN A SEAT closer to his regular spot—he was anxious for everyone to have a say and Susan's contribution the previous week had been a real boost to the discussion. He also noticed a few new faces at the tables that had been pushed together into their meeting circle and thought to himself, *My, my, we seem to be gathering a bit of steam.* He smiled at Susan as he kicked off the evening's discussion.

"Last Monday, I suggested that we think about the scope and history of the responsible versus irresponsible issue," he said.

Barbara was ready for him. "At my office, there's a feeling that society has changed and is headed in the direction of irresponsibility," she said. "It seems to be the exception rather than the rule when an employee who knows right from wrong when faced with a challenging situation makes the choice to do the right thing. For example, employees who use the company's phone for personal calls during working hours know that they're getting less work done. The employees also know that using the company's phone costs the company money, and there is a clear company policy about the improper use of phones for personal reasons.

"Nowadays," Barbara continued, "the use of people's own cell phones doesn't raise the company's phone bill, but it still impacts productivity when workers are making cell phone calls during working hours, instead of waiting for lunch or break time. All the employees know this slows us down. From the perspective of a good work ethic, it's wrong to commit such an act."

"Yet, people do this all the time," said Ellen.

"Exactly," said Joe. "This gives us some indication of the scope of the irresponsible behavior issue." Then, he asked, "Let me see the hands of those who have seen irresponsible behavior displayed in your workplace because there's no consistent application of company policy." The response was unanimous—everyone in the group raised a hand.

"There's a second part to this question," Joe continued. "Raise your hand if you've seen irresponsible behavior displayed in your workplace resulting from employees having a lack of respect for company policy?" Again, the show of hands was unanimous.

"Your response yielded similar results to an informal survey I conducted recently. The survey asked people to respond to this question: 'Do you feel that today's society is shifting more toward a responsible or an irresponsible behavioral environment?' The results suggested that most people believe today's society is shifting toward an irresponsible society," Joe explained.

"Giving examples of irresponsible behaviors is easy in today's world," said Ellen. "The frequency of examples is a problem within itself," she suggested.

"I agree with how repeatedly these irresponsible situations can be cited," said Joe. "Two important questions should be addressed: What events influence our attitudes to a point of refusing to take responsibility for our own behavior? And what are the internal and external events that help shift the workplace toward a less responsible behavioral environment?

"The external events are changes in societal attitudes or sentiments that apply to everyone in their lives outside of work. Examples like no-fault auto insurance and no-fault divorce come to mind. And government pardons for criminals that have committed known crimes is another example. That is like saying the crime was acceptable behavior.

"In contrast, there are internal events controlled within the corporate, federal, state, and local government workplaces. Last week we spoke of a case of management personnel who do not lead by modeling responsible behavior—when an absentee policy is applied to the non-management workforce and not to management. This strategy puts the company at risk of tilting the behavioral environment toward irresponsibility."

"It seems like the American attitude has gone from *the buck stops here*, to a point where passing the buck and blaming others when things go wrong is fashionable," responded Susan. "But most people don't hesitate to take credit when things go right.

"I think the no-fault examples Joe mentioned have existed since the 1960s. This no-fault attitude has crept into society at large, including the places we work," Susan continued. "For example, no-fault auto insurance supports a mentality of denying that the car crash ever happened, because neither driver's actions caused the car accident. Yet, the reality is that the cars—what Joe would call the 'non-living objects' in this situation, right?" Joe nodded agreement as she went on. "The cars cannot cause an accident without the people who are driving them. The same can be said for no-fault divorce. If neither husband nor wife is at fault, then why is there a divorce proceeding?"

"And then there are people suing individuals or corporations for their own blunders," added Ellen. "Like suing fast food chains and cigarette companies because you're a smoker and get cancer or you end up with diabetes because of obesity from bad eating habits. Some people have even attempted to sue the gun makers when their products have injured or killed someone. We all know that a gun is a non-living object that cannot kill without the actions of a human being.

"A similar case can be made for food causing obesity," Ellen continued. "Knowledge has provided us with a simple formula for controlling our weight—input equals output! Food alone does not cause obesity—a person's failure to eat responsibly causes obesity.

And when it comes to my kids, it's my responsibility to feed them healthy food, not a steady diet of food from fast food chains'!"

"But what about the cultural factors related to obesity?" asked Edward, absent-mindedly patting his own well-rounded middle.

"Granted," Greg responded "But no matter what kind of culture you grew up in, you still have a choice. My family was poor, and while I was growing up, eating healthy foods to control weight was not the top priority. Having enough food, period, was the top priority. Later, when I learned more about the importance of the kind of food I ate, how much I ate, and getting physical activity, I developed enough awareness to control my weight."

"The buck gets passed for lack of success everywhere in life," Barbara commented. "It happens in business, politics, religion, the educational system, governments, and personal relationships," she went on. "Holding people responsible for their actions is getting tougher every day. In legal matters, we attempt to hold people responsible all the time, even if they end up getting away with something. With morality, on the other hand, it's as though no one is responsible for what they do. And it's that awareness and acting from knowing the difference between right and wrong that makes somebody a moral person! It seems so obvious," Barbara lamented, "It's what determines a person's character!"

Most of the people in the group were shaking their heads in agreement with Barbara, clearly distressed by this observation. "Most people have a set of moral principles," Joe said gently. "Religion is not necessarily required for these moral principles to exist, as they are merely a defined standard of right and wrong. Although there is a tendency to apply a moral construct to the judicial system, there is a difference between being legal and being moral."

The room was quiet for a few minutes as everyone thought about how this difference applied to them. For Greg, an African American, many images from the history of his people came to mind. Susan's religion was a central part of her life, and these notions of good and bad, and legal versus moral behavior were often on her mind. Ellen, as a security guard, was well aware of such conundrums. "How so?" she asked.

"For example, apartheid was legal in South Africa for many decades," Joe replied, "But its violation of human rights was wrong and immoral. In today's behavioral environment, religious-based moral laws have been replaced by the judicial system as the standard to guide us in our decisions. Trying to mix moral laws with the judicial system is one of the reasons our courts are filled with frivolous lawsuits. People are always trying to have their cake and eat it too.

"In this country, for example," Joe continued, "in order for the police to search your property, a valid search warrant authorized by a judge is necessary. But suppose that the police acted overzealously, didn't have a valid search warrant, still proceeded to search private property, and found illegal drugs. The person in possession of the drugs is clearly morally guilty, but the police violated that person's irrefutable rights of privacy.

"So, in order to protect the person's rights—and yours and mine— the court would disallow the drugs as evidence in a trial. If the drugs were the only facts the court had linking the person with the crime, then the case would be dismissed. The person is legally considered to be not guilty." As he said this he noticed one of the new people half raising his hand.

"Welcome," Joe said, smiling at the middle-aged man, taking in that he had draped the jacket of his handsome gray suit over the back of his chair.

"Hi," the man responded. "I'm Stewart. My wife works at the airport in one of the gift shops and heard about these meetings. I hope it's okay I stopped by."

Susan turned and waved to him, "Hi! Welcome, of course it's okay. We'll have to talk before we leave so you can tell me who your wife is—I work in a gift shop there, too. Where do you work, Stewart?"

"I guess I'm what you'd call a 'middle manager' in a printing company," Stewart replied. "I'm really interested in how to get people moving in a more responsible direction at work. Everyone seems to be unaware of what goes on inside people that causes a reaction in the environment, or of the consequences and learning that should follow."

Joe was impressed, as he was with all of the people participating in this coffee shop conversation. He said, "Indeed, welcome, Stewart, your comments are right in line with what we're trying to understand in order to bring some new ideas about responsibility into all of our workplaces. The rationale for our reactions to company policies and procedures, as well as life in general, usually comes down to common sense choices.

"Some examples already mentioned in our discussions include showing up to work on time, performing tasks to the best of your abilities, having the courage to do the right thing, and treating others as you want to be treated. Why would people risk short-term rewards over long-term consequences by reacting irresponsibly to situations that might have such negative impact on their lives? This is the problem, both at our jobs and in everyday life, which affects all human beings. There really doesn't have to be unresolved corporate corruption, bankruptcy, and low productivity in the workplace—there is a choice. The first step in resolving these problems is being accountable for your own actions and inactions," he concluded.

"Yes," Stewart responded, quickly being drawn into the discussion, "but the track record for resolving these issues leaves much to be desired. It seems as if our society has become immune to the world's issues, and we have accepted the fact that these problems are part of life—that things will always be this way. There seems to be a lack of urgency to figure out the root cause of the problems. And when someone does dig up some real insight into the causes of major problems in our society, the media and government often turn a deaf ear."

"I realize that," said Joe, "but the benefits of dealing directly with these problems can have a huge positive impact on the behavioral environment of future generations.

"People who have built a reputation for acting responsibly are trusted to do things on their own. Being trusted is a good feeling, and it's a win-win situation for employer and employee, or parent and child. Trust builds self-esteem and self-worth for children and adults alike.

40

"An employee who is trusted will be given tasks of greater responsibility, which will then lead to recognition, pay raises, and promotions. A business that has a reputation for being responsible to their customers will gain leadership in its market.

"Likewise, politicians who can be trusted to act in the best interests of their constituents and not sell out to special interest groups, or say just anything to get elected, will usually get elected or re-elected," Joe added.

"So, the bottom line is that awareness of the human behavior process is the key for shifting society toward more responsibility," Greg suggested.

"If we know the root cause of the problem, we should be able to fix that problem," Joe said.

The group was so engrossed in conversation that they had lost track of time. It was after seven p.m., and they had to bring their coffee shop gathering to a close.

The regulars sat in silence for several minutes. Everyone was reflecting on the views that had been discussed. They were beginning to realize that the picture painted during their discussion of responsible and irresponsible behavior held key factors for success and failure. Human behavior is the common bond not only in business and government environments, but is also at the core of all other environments created and controlled by humans. Using a direct, common sense approach makes understanding the issue much simpler.

The group had made significant progress in getting their minds around the issue. They had defined the problem, identified the connecting issues, determined the scope, and gotten insight into the past and current situations. The question was specific and simple: **How did behavior shift from responsible toward irresponsible actions?** As for the answer, **the awareness of the importance of human accountability** was beginning to make its full impact on the group.

Armed with an improved understanding of the problem, they knew something had to be done to fix it. Solving the problem could make the world a better place. "**How?**" remained the big question.

"There are always two sides to a problem," Barbara said, putting on her coat. "If people are consistently responsible for their actions, they are still challenged by their surroundings—willpower is tested all the time. On the other hand, those who act irresponsibly have to be challenged to be more accountable."

"You're right," said Joe. "It's a matter of people looking into the mirror and asking themselves the question: 'Who do you really see in the mirror?' and deciding whether to behave responsibly or irresponsibly. This gives me an idea for our next discussion.

"So far, we have described responsible and irresponsible behavior and cited some real life examples. We have also identified external and internal actions that have influenced the workplace behavioral environment. I suggest that we identify common sense principles of responsible behavior for our next gathering. These principles, if adopted, will help guide employees toward responsible action or inactions when reacting to situations. We need at least four volunteers to come up with three principles each of responsible behavior and present them to the group. And I'll volunteer to be one of those four."

The "I'll do it!" responses drowned each other out and people started to laugh. "All right!" Joe said in a celebratory tone, resisting the urge to punch his fist in the air. "You folks are so great. How about we go with Edward, Ellen and Brian for this one—trust me, there will be plenty for all of you to do before we're done!" Joe had purposefully chosen some of the less vocal members of the group to give them a chance to have their say. He was uplifted by the energy coming from these hardworking people, giving time they could have been spending at home to try and make their workplaces, and, yes, the world, more responsible and healthier for everyone.

"As each of you prepares to go to work, stop and look into your mirror, and take the time to ask this question: 'Who do I really see in the mirror?' Then, try to see beyond your physical appearance and examine your internal being before going through your daily activities at work. Pay particular attention to your feelings, thoughts, actions, and inactions as you try to identify the principles of responsible behavior—the rules applied to guide your behavior in workplace situations or personal life. The second part of this as-

42

signment is for you to think of a benefit that follows when you apply the principles of responsible behavior."

As checks were handed out, one of the servers said, "I always enjoy your group's discussions, especially on such an important topic as being responsible. Apparently, I'm not the only one—our business is beginning to pick up, and I noticed that some of our customers who are always on the go are hanging around to listen. I'm a single parent of a teenage boy, and sometimes he can be responsible, and at other times, boy, can he be irresponsible. I tell him that employers are looking for people who are responsible. I tell him some things from your talks, like the fact that behavior seems to be the key to all successes and failures."

"Yes," Joe replied. "It's like having a coin that has responsible on one side and irresponsible on the other. What both sides have in common is behavior."

CHAPTER Four

Twelve Common Sense Principles of Responsible Behavior

WHEN JOE AND THE REGULARS ARRIVED THE NEXT MONDAY, THEY EN-gaged in their usual small talk, catching up with each other's weekly activities. The volunteers who had identified principles of responsible behavior were eager to get into the heart of the discussion. The coffee shop was full of customers who had heard about the group's gathering. This time, the audience was mixed with regulars and several new customers.

Joe opened the discussion. "At our last gathering, I suggested that four of us each come up with three principles of responsible behavior and the expected benefits of applying these principles. Who would like to begin?"

Ellen stood up with an obvious combination of nervousness and excitement. "Hi, I'm Ellen. I'm a security guard at the airport and I'm a single mom—my kids are 11 and 15. Like Joe said we should, every day during last week, I looked in the mirror to see beyond my physical appearance, and tried to see my internal being—which I guess I personally think of as, well, my soul. Then, I asked the question: 'Who do you see in the mirror?'"

...n had paid particular attention ...ons when she responded to situa-

...ehavior that represents the corner- ...s honesty," she suggested. So this is

...f and others in both words and actions.

...sistently by this principle, they earn the ...nesty builds self-esteem, character, and ...s considered trustworthy, and able to carry ...and duties."

...ne shop as people responded to Ellen's ...e so many people in the room, Susan ...hand. Ellen smiled at the classroom-like ...agree," Susan said, "that the principle of ...rtant character trait a person can possess. But it's idealistic ...gine that we live in a perfect world—frankly, I doubt if most people today apply honesty consistently in every situation. I mean, I recognize that many people do indeed live by this principle, but I also think their choice of behavior depends on the situation.

"Like, if you work where the culture is not supportive of honesty, employees will be reluctant to be honest. I mean, suppose an organization has a policy of terminating workers after making only one unintentional mistake—one strike and you're out. Under such a strict condition, workers wouldn't be honest about admitting mistakes. The need for job security and stability would make honesty a real risk."

"If honesty is in the fiber of a person's character," Greg said, "then applying the principle based on circumstances shouldn't be the determining factor. The truth should always be based on facts, regardless of the situation or the consequences of telling the truth."

"The world would certainly be a better place to live, if everyone adopted the principle of 'being honest with yourself and others in both words and actions,'" added Stewart. "But in the real world, that's just not the deal."

"Honesty," said Joe, "is not uniquely tied to the workplace behavioral environment; it must also be applied in our daily lives. Honesty is connected to all of our relationships, like family, friends, marriage, and community. Honesty is a universal principle that should be adopted and applied in all walks of life. If individuals, as members of a community, are going to shift society toward an environment of responsible behavior, then they must start with themselves. The most direct way to come face-to-face with the reality of one's self is by looking into your mirror daily, and confronting the reflection with the question, 'am I part of the problem or part of the solution?' Then, we can all become active participants in a responsible behavior movement by modeling honesty in everything we do."

"Good point, Joe," replied Ellen. "Well, it seems we could talk about honesty all night and day—but here's my second principle and the expected benefits:

Principle II: Be publicly accountable for your own actions and inactions.

Benefits: Trust, confidence, and respect for self and others are earned by being accountable. Being accountable shows true leadership, dependability and reliability. Being accountable displays self-discipline, commitment, pride, and a positive attitude in completing the task.

Ellen nodded at Stewart to speak next." If everyone lived life based on this principle of responsible behavior," he explained, "we would not be having this discussion today. Being publicly accountable for ones own actions and inactions is like saying that you do exist and are valued. In contrast, not being publicly accountable is like saying that you do not exist, or that you don't have self-ownership.

"Accountability for your own actions or inactions in response to the environment," Stewart continued, "can only be owned by the person who committed the actual act. However, there are certain situations where the ownership of an action is shared. For example, a child should not be the only one held responsible for what he or she does—the parents must share part of the responsibility for their child's actions. It's the parents' job to teach their children about responsibility, right from wrong, consequences, learning, and acceptable and unacceptable behavior. They are also the ones that must reinforce those behaviors by modeling what they want their children to learn."

"Identifying behavioral principles that people should adopt to guide their actions is the easy part," interjected Barbara. "Getting people to embrace such principles and integrate them into the fiber of their beings is the difficult part. Reactions to any situation in the environment become conditioned by experience.

"For example, if a person took responsibility for a decision that resulted in a company's loss of millions of dollars, the consequence should involve learning by experiencing the outcome. Some people have the self-confidence, courage, honesty, and leadership skills to admit their mistakes and learn from them. However, it's unrealistic to think that all people will behave like this."

Joe asked a rhetorical question. "Why is it that some people don't take responsibility for their actions? Being responsible for one's own behavior seems clear-cut in my opinion."

"Besides the obvious lack of confidence in one's self," replied Susan, "I think the underlying reason for not taking responsibility for your own actions is the fear of the consequences, and how the outcome will be seen by others."

"Another reason people don't take responsibility for their own actions," added Ellen, "is because it's easy these days to blame other influences. It's pretty outrageous how much of that goes on—and I'm only talking about the stuff we know about from the news! Scandal, corruption, disrespect for human life, prejudice, senseless acts of violence, self-centeredness, and immorality are more common than ever. Especially when governments, corporations, schools, and church leaders are caught being so irresponsible, one has to wonder, where are the positive role models?"

"Exactly," said Joe. "You are describing the collective mindset— the opinions and morals—of individuals that are understood to be part of the current culture.

"But it isn't hopeless, really!" he continued. "A way to move forward in reversing the trends just described is to understand the internal factors that are influencing people to behave the way they do. Understanding the internal factors is like looking into our car's rear view mirror to remind us where we have been or what is behind us. There is a great deal already known about people's internal needs, and the actions and choices that satisfy those needs."

"What would you say are people's internal needs? Are you talking about things like food and love?" asked Brian.

"People have a need for safety, security, and stability," responded Joe, "as well as for belonging, love, respect, acceptance, and self-fulfillment. But we only get to the psychological needs of belonging, love, respect, acceptance and self-fulfillment once the basic physiological needs to sustain life, like air, water, food, sex, shelter, etc., are satisfied. Seeking to satisfy these needs influences people's actions based on the circumstances they are in at a particular moment.

"Once the basic physiological needs are satisfied, people will focus on the safety and security of being out of danger. Then come the psychological needs. It has been well documented that psychological needs are used to justify responsible and irresponsible behavior.

"Psychological needs are subconscious," he stated, "but they still have influence over human behavior. In an attempt to gratify these natural built-in psychological needs, people seek pleasure and satisfaction to avoid pain and stress. If the experience learned from an action results in pleasure or satisfaction, people become conditioned, and they will repeat that behavior in response to future similar situations. Likewise, if the experience learned from an action is pain or stress, they will be conditioned to avoid behaving in that manner in the future.

"Some people are aware and are in touch with the root causes that conditioned their behavior to satisfy their psychological needs, some are not aware or in touch and others remain in a state of denial.

"The solution to modifying behavior is to understand and get in touch with psychological or social needs. In addition, people must understand how human behavior operates when they do what they do to satisfy these needs. This awareness can help people avoid irresponsible behavior.

48

"In my view," Joe continued, "if people have a need for belonging, respect, and acceptance, it doesn't make sense to risk jeopardizing getting those needs met by not being accountable for your behavior—unless the act to satisfy these needs is in conflict with the principle of responsible behavior.

"Here's an example: A person has the need to belong and to be accepted into a workplace team. The leader of the team comes up with an idea that is both unethical and unlawful. In this situation, the person's need to belong and to be accepted as part of the work team will have some influence on the choice that person makes. It comes down to satisfying the need to belong and to be accepted, and therefore give in to enticement and deal with the stress of not doing what the person believes to be right. It would be a no-brainer for some to reject this irresponsible behavior, but in today's workplace environment, some employees would risk their careers to satisfy the need to belong and to be accepted over showing that they know right from wrong.

"Being accountable for one's own behavior to satisfy human psychological needs should not be the major concern. The concern," Joe explained, "should be about what type of behavior people are willing to display to satisfy these needs. This was pointed out in Ellen's second principle of responsible behavior. I recognize the fact that people do have a real fear of not belonging or being accepted— it's a natural social feeling.

"However, the fear does not justify an irresponsible response to a situation when dealing with that fear. It seems as if we are looking for an excuse to blame others for our own actions. As we've said before, today's society is beginning to shift more toward an irresponsible behavior environment. Resisting the influences of irresponsible actions and modeling responsible behavior is a way to reverse the shift."

"Well," interjected Ellen, "again, we could go on for a very long time with this discussion about being accountable for one's actions, but I want to present my third principle, which is closely related to the first and second."

Principle III: Admit your mistakes. It is better to lose face than to save face on false pretenses.

Benefits: Admitting mistakes is being honest with yourself. Admitting errors builds others' confidence in you.

"Most people know that the consequences of mistakes will cause distress," she continued. "Even though people have a tendency to avoid emotional pain, it's better to face the music without delay. Honesty is the backbone of admitting mistakes and having confidence in yourself, regardless of the outcome. These are key character traits a person should possess."

"People are imperfect by nature and thus, mistakes are expected. However, people must learn from the consequences of their mistakes. This is crucial in improving further behavioral situations.

"A prime example of admitting your mistake and the resulting consequences is a situation in the work place where a mistake you make costs the company money. This can be very embarrassing. I remember the time I was scheduled for an advanced training program on airport security. The training was out of town and my travel plans had to be changed at the very last minute. My boss asked me if I needed help making the necessary changes to the travel arrangements and I declined the offer indicating that I had everything under control.

"Later I learned I had forgotten to change the hotel reservations. The company had to pay for the first night's stay even though I was not there that night. I was embarrassed to admit to my boss that the company was being charged for my mistake and tried to think of ways around it so he would not know. In the end I told him about the mistake and apologized for making the error. That one taught me not only to check all the details when making travel plans but also to accept help when it is offered by others who know more than you about a task. I am pleased to say I have never made that same mistake again."

Joe acknowledged Ellen's contribution and noted that Edward and Brian were anxious to give their presentations, but the time for bringing the gathering to a close was approaching. Joe glanced at his watch. "We may only have enough time to present one or two more principles, depending on the discussion that follows."

Edward rose and said, "I'll go next. The principles that I thought about when I looked into the mirror were about three traits of responsibility. These are courage, placing blame, and being proactive. My first principle and its expected benefits are:

Principle IV: Have the courage to do the right thing, especially when confronted with a difficult situation that challenges your strength of character.

Benefits: You display bravery, justice, and fairness. You practice unbiased and fair treatment for all human beings regardless of race, gender or economic status.

"If honesty is the most important character trait a person possesses," he said, "then courage is the next most important trait. Admitting your mistakes, even though the consequences will be stressful, requires courage. My first thought when I am placed in that situation is to avoid stress by not admitting to the mistake. This is a natural human reaction. We all want to step away from a mess and pretend we didn't see it, much less admit we did it. However, doing the right thing tends to overrule that thought, especially if the mistake impacts others."

"How do you deal with the pressure of being exposed to irresponsible behavior when co-workers do not admit to their mistakes?" Joe asked.

"Co-workers' not admitting to their mistakes is so frustrating," Edward answered. "But having a sense of who I am, and knowing my own comfort zone, provides the strength I need to resist falling into the trap of acting irresponsibly."

Greg spoke up, and it was clear from his expression and tone of voice that he had some doubts. "How could a person resist following a crowd who doesn't admit their mistakes?" he asked. "I think a person who follows their conscience instead of the crowd is rare today. Your courage to admit your mistakes might really blow your relationships with co-workers who aren't into that, don't you think?" he asked.

"I wish I could have taken a poll on what co-workers think about admitting to mistakes," responded Edward, "but I have had some co-workers say that they admire and respect a person who displays courage when facing difficult situations."

Edward glanced at the clock over the coffee shop counter and looked around to see if there were more questions. "It really is getting late, so I'm going to get right to my next principle. It focuses on playing the blame game. My next principle and its expected benefits are:

Principle V: Do not blame others for the consequences of your actions and inactions.

Benefits: Accepting responsibility for your actions and inactions is a sign of genuine leadership. It demonstrates objectivity in resolving issues. You do not become distracted by accusing others.

"Today, playing the blame game is a really common way of avoiding being responsible for one's own actions. Not playing the game is a direct and clear-cut choice," Edward explained.

"I agree that it's a good principle to live by," said Susan, "but I can't imagine an environment or society free of placing blame."

"Why not?" asked Joe. "Generally, we know how and why people behave when reacting to situations in the environment."

"How so?" asked Stewart.

Joe answered, "People tend to seek pleasure or satisfaction and avoid pain or stress. At work, employees seek tasks they like doing and avoid tasks that they do not like doing, or that they find boring. The tasks people like provide pleasure—the state of being satisfied—and the tasks they do not like provide pain or stress—the state of being dissatisfied. So, many people blame others to avoid inflicting emotional stress or physical pain on themselves. They respond to their fear of losing a sense of belonging, acceptance, respect, love, self-confidence, and so on."

"Can seeking pleasure and avoiding pain be applied to any situation?" asked Susan.

"Yes," replied Joe, "the behavioral rule can be applied to work, activities, events, people, relationships, etc. Some people are conscious of why and how they behave the way they do, and others are not aware. The longer a person behaves in a certain manner that establishes a pattern, the less likely they are to be aware of how they behave. People become mesmerized with behavior that falls into a pattern to the extent that it diminishes their conscious awareness."

"Why is that?" asked Barbara, who was taking careful notes, as she did through all the discussions. Joe had noticed this and knew there would come a time when he would be calling upon her to share her conscientiously filled notebook.

"After behaving in a certain way, guided by the experience of pleasure or pain, people create a comfort zone," responded Joe. "In other words, they become conditioned, and are less likely to be conscious of how they behave. Conscious thinking about their actions is reduced. It's like putting behavior on automatic pilot. This is why having principles to help guide responsible behavior is an important factor. One person's pleasure can be another person's pain, or vice-versa."

Edward looked up at the clock again, and said, "I hate to end this discussion—it's got us going pretty good! But I'm going to have to wait until next Monday to share my third principal."

Joe nodded and smiled at the obvious high level of involvement in the evening's discussion. "Edward's right—we really do have to stop now. Let me just summarize a bit: We have heard five principles and benefits of responsible behaviors. These five principles covered honesty, accountability, admitting to mistakes, courage, and not placing blame. Next week, we'll start with the remaining principle in Edward's presentation. It has been a pleasure to see so many new faces, and I hope we'll see all of you again next Monday."

As usual, Joe and the regulars showed up at five p.m. the following Monday. As Joe was getting ready to start the discussion, he noticed that the coffee shop was again filled with more newcomers who had heard about the discussions. The audience was mixed with old and young, male and female, people from all walks of life.

At the previous gathering, Edward had cited honesty and accountability as two character traits of people who behave responsibly. Joe quickly reiterated these principles and introduced Edward.

"My next principle of responsible behavior centers on the character trait of being proactive," began Edward. "Like the previous principles, it is clear-cut and based on common sense.

"The principle and its expected benefits are:

Principle VI: Be proactive. Consider the consequences of your actions before initiating them.

Benefits: Planning ahead shows rational behavior and can prevent mistakes that you will later regret. It earns you the reputation for making sound judgments instead of being impulsive, emotional, and reactionary.

"Using the expression 'What were you thinking?' is common when someone at work or in life performs an irresponsible act," Edward said. "The most common response to that question when a person acts irresponsibly is 'I don't know—I guess I wasn't thinking.'

"An incident my neighbor told me that happened in her office demonstrates this. An employee stealing on the job was captured on camera while performing the theft. The outcome was that an employee who badly needed a job was fired for the incident. Practicing the proactive principle would have helped this person avoid being put into the position of being asked, 'What were you thinking?' Being proactive requires you to think about the consequences before taking the action."

"Many workers react on impulse rather than giving thought to consequences," Greg commented. "I'm wondering how that behavior will ever change."

"I agree that in the real world getting people to think before they act would be a difficult task," replied Edward. "We would, of course, not expect infants and children to avoid impulsive behavior—otherwise, we probably wouldn't all have heard someone say, 'what were you thinking?'" he concluded to some welcome laughter from the audience.

"Difficult, yes, impossible, no," said Joe. "People are in control of themselves and hold the power to change their own behavior. The mindset that causes people to react spontaneously to a situation before they think can be changed. This is done by getting in touch with the root cause that brought about the impulsive behavior," he explained.

"I agree that impulsive, negative behavior can be changed," said Edward. "I think we are headed in the right direction for coming up with a solution."

Not wanting time to run out, Joe quickly asked Brian to share his three principles. "I sense that the audience is anxious to hear the remaining principles. So, if the group would hold off on the discussion until Brian has completed all three principles, we can speed things up," Joe suggested.

The others agreed.

Brian stood up and cleared his throat. He was quick with a quip, and used to talking to the guests at the hotel where he worked. Speaking about a serious topic in front of a group of attentive listeners was new to him. But he was proud of the work he had done, and remembered how often confidence had been mentioned as a trait worth having. "So," he began, "my first principle and its benefits are:

Principle VII: Do not seek pleasure by inflicting pain on others.

Benefit: Sensitivity and concern for the well being of others are learned behavior, as is selflessness. Demonstrating sensitivity earns the respect of others.

"Earlier, we talked about how people seek pleasure and avoid pain," continued Brian. "This particular behavioral rule applies to almost everything people do. Some examples were given such as work, activities, events, relationships, etc. Seeking pleasure is a natural internal response. But, this behavior can be misused when your pleasure becomes someone else's pain.

"For example," he explained, "not carrying your share of the workload may give you pleasure at the expense of causing pain for your co-workers. The co-worker who does his or her share and your share of the workload will become frustrated and resentful. I'm also sure that this type of behavior doesn't only happen at work. It happens in other surroundings—at home, in our families and in all kinds of organizations." Brian felt better now that he had started talking, and looked to Joe for agreement that he should go on. Joe nodded.

As he began to speak, Brian realized how he had used the next principle himself to speak to this group. "I have to tell you," he said, smiling, "that just putting these principles in writing and sharing them with you has already changed my behavior—and those are words that I previously have associated with my report cards at school when I was a kid". Making a silly face and raising his voice to a falsetto, he said "Brian would do well to restrain from his distracting behavior in my classroom. He's a good boy, but…" The laughter at this was just what he needed to feel more relaxed. Shaking off the silliness with a toss of his head, Brian continued. "My second principle and its benefits are:

Principle VIII: Take full ownership of your actions.

Benefits: Others will respect you because you are self-confident, a strong leader, and have a strong character. This builds self-worth.

"One of things I thought of while working on this principle is the behavior of children," Brian added. "An infant or young child owns his or her actions even though his parents are responsible for the child. The parents didn't actually commit the act—only one person can do that, so the child owns the act. But because the child lacks maturity, parents are held responsible for their child's actions.

"Another thing that came to mind is how people are more focused today on building wealth based on material possessions rather than on good character traits. I mean, how many of the reality TV shows on now are all about pursuing money? When you look at the huge number of people watching these shows, you've got to ask that question!"

Feeling pleased with his presentation so far, Brian forged on. "My third principle and its benefits are:

Principle IX: Pursue your own well being while respecting the needs of others and laws.

Benefit: You gain a high regard for the well being of yourself, others, and the legal system.

"I think that most people are sensitive to the needs of others," Greg responded. "But, there sure are some who are self-absorbed, and they have an 'it's all about me' attitude. Maybe, if those who are sensitive to the needs of others modeled their selfless behavior, their example could help influence those who are not."

"The influence factor works both ways," Ellen suggested. "The people who are self-absorbed seem to influence those who are sensitive."

Joe explained, "There are always two options of behavior to choose from: selfish or selfless. The good news is that behavior is something we control. Thus, it can be fixed. It's a matter of asking yourself the question, 'Who do you really see in the mirror?' Do you reveal a selfless or selfish character? Before you answer, use the principle of being honest with yourself and others in both words and actions. If your answer is selfish, then seek a common sense self-help tool to fix it."

"Why do you suggest the self-help tool approach instead of getting professional help?" asked Barbara.

"Both approaches will work," Joe answered. "However, the self-help approach is what I recommend, because I believe that the greater part of improving oneself depends on the individual, regardless of whether or not you consult a professional. The individual has to decide if he or she needs and wants to be helped. This is the biggest hurdle. Once a person has overcome that obstacle, change is only a matter of using the proper self-help tool to aid in focusing and guiding the person's efforts."

The volunteers had described their three principles of responsible behavior and the benefits one can expect from adopting them as part of ones values. Joe had yet to share his three principles with the group. He looked at his watch, and said, "Time has gone by quickly. I have given my three principles considerable thought. As I listened to the nine principles presented so well by our volunteers, I discovered, just as they did, that the principles are simply common sense choices applied when people respond to situations in the workplace and in life.

"Some people have a tendency to over-analyze situations, instead of keeping things simple. Many times the solutions to problems are so obvious that we cannot see them. Or, in other cases, people are in a state of denial and don't want to face the solution. We are often blinded by other distractions in the behavioral environment that interfere with direct focus on the root cause. The issue of responsible and irresponsible human behavior must be addressed directly. Development of principles of responsible behavior is a vital element in doing so.

"Unfortunately, there really isn't enough time left to share my three principles, so I'll do that at the next gathering so we're not rushed." Joe concluded.

By the time Monday rolled around again, the word had continued to spread about the coffee shop gatherings. Joe and the regulars had taken on the challenge of making the workplace a more responsible environment. The issue of responsible behavior created an interest amongst many of the local workers, and once again, there were more new faces in the audience.

Though Joe had not yet arrived, the patrons had moved the tables and chairs and were seated and ready to go. Stewart stood and said, "I'm sorry to sound skeptical, but can such a critical factor as human behavior be changed? After all, responsible human behavior has been addressed over time with some degree of both success and failure, but the idea of taking on the workforce seems, well, for lack of a better word, a bit grandiose."

Barbara was shaking her head. As Stewart sat down, she said, "I disagree, Stewart. I really think looking at the behavioral environments where we work is the only way to change the problem of irresponsible behavior. People trying to change irresponsible behavior on their own, just by themselves, would probably only result in short term success. What I believe is that all people are connected by their behavior, regardless of age, gender, culture, race, or religion. Without addressing the behavioral environment as a whole, I don't think much long term, sustainable improvement in people's responsible behavior would be possible."

"Phew, you guys are raring to go, huh?" commented Greg. "I wonder if Joe got stuck in front of his mirror."

Joe walked into the pleasant sound of the group chuckling over Greg's remark. "No," he said, taking a seat, "I didn't get stuck, but I did have a long conversation with my mirror, and the oddest thing happened. I kept waiting for the person I saw to say something. That moment helped me to look deep inside to come up with the three principles of responsible behavior I'm going to share with you.

"Often when humans try to resolve problems, we make the problem seem more difficult than it really is. We inflict ourselves with unnecessary emotions instead of facing the problem directly and keeping it simple. My first principle and its benefits are based on plain and simple common sense acts.

Principle X: Learn from the consequences of your actions and inactions.
Benefit: Being aware of the consequences will help you avoid mistakes in the future.

"If being honest with oneself and others in both words and actions is the most important principle," Joe continued, "and the courage to do what's right is the second, then learning from the consequences of ones actions would be the next most important principle."

"I agree," interjected the interjection-prone Barbara, "that learning from the consequences of your actions is one of the most important principles a person must apply to demonstrate responsible behavior. But what about situations where people keep repeating the same bad behavior?

"For example, even though an employee clearly understands the absentee policy, he is surprised when his supervisor brings up his high absentee rate during a performance review. He's given a warning that he's told is going into his personnel file. After the performance review, his absentee rate went down, but only for a few months, and then it went back up. Obviously, this employee did not learn from the consequence of his actions.

"Another example," continued Barbara "is the CEOs who misled investors, then renounced their responsibilities, were caught and forced to face justice. Yet, we are still faced with other CEOs making the same mistakes as those who were caught. The CEOs who continue to be corrupt in light of those caught sends the message that corruption is okay, just don't get caught. And if you do get caught, blame others for your actions. Instead, CEOs should learn from the consequences of those who were prosecuted that corruption is wrong, irresponsible, and unacceptable. If you choose to be corrupt, there are consequences, and you will be held accountable."

Barbara needed to take a breath, and Greg jumped in, saying, "Likewise, government officials at high levels are still making the same corrupt decisions, yet several government officials have been caught, prosecuted, and sentenced for their crimes. Again, like the heads of those companies Barbara was talking about, it appears that there is no learning from the consequences of others even though several people have been caught and have actually gone to jail."

Stewart commented, "I am amazed that some employers still fail to take quick action to deal directly with employees who behave irresponsibly at work—the ones who fail to do their fair share of work, are always blaming others, and show disrespect for themselves, their co-workers, rules, and property."

"It's a big problem in businesses today," Joe replied. "Such workers are often constantly unhappy, and may even be unstable. Disgruntled, they are certainly more likely than fulfilled, well-adjusted employees to provoke discontent and possibly even violence in the workplace. Employers who are aware of employees with that kind of profile, but take no action to correct the situation, are continuing to abdicate their responsibility. As a result, there is no learning to be found because of the employer's failure to act.

"Employees who perform their tasks year after year and make the same mistakes repeatedly do not learn from the consequences of their actions," Joe continued. "This type of performance occurs frequently among both management and non-management personnel. For me it brings to mind the difference between an employee who has ten years of experience and the one who has one year's worth of the same experiences repeated ten times.

"The former has learned from the consequences of his or her actions and inactions over the course of the ten years. This employee does not keep making the same mistakes. On the other hand, the latter keeps making the same mistakes year in and year out and does not learn from the consequences of his or her actions over the ten years. Though both employees may have the same total number of years with a company, the lessons learned account for the differences between the performances of the two."

Ellen spoke up then. "A lot of employees these days seem to think they just won't get caught committing an unethical or corrupt act. Their view is that others got caught because they weren't smart enough. Or, they think no one is going to notice that they're not doing their fair share of work. Besides, they figure, there are other employees who are not doing their fair share."

"Or, if leadership personnel ignore the issue of irresponsible employees," added Stewart, "they mistakenly believe that the problem or the employee will eventually go away or self-correct. Meanwhile, management doesn't realize the serious damage done by these people. Their negative behavior is affecting the morale and productivity of the whole workforce. Once this is allowed to continue with no consequences, the situation can reach a point where the problem becomes irreversible.

"I've seen it happen in places where I've worked. Productive employees with good work ethics can't counterbalance the problem unless the behavior of the irresponsible workers is eliminated. And I also think the employers are responsible for correcting the problem, so to solve the problem, often the company has to get rid of some top management personnel.

"What is disconcerting about the principle 'learn from the consequence of your actions,'" continued Stewart, "is that there are people who do not apply this principle to guide their actions at work or in their daily lives. People aren't perfect, and we don't live in a perfect world. We expect and understand that human actions will sometimes result in mistakes. What is difficult to understand is that when people make mistakes, some don't learn from the consequences and then avoid making the same mistakes in the future."

"How shocking do the acts and consequences have to be in the behavioral environment before people learn from their actions?" asked Susan. "The September 11, 2000 terrorist attacks on the World Trade Center shocked the world. But if the right people had learned from the first World Trade Center attack, the second attack might never have happened."

"I'm hoping learning can take place from the consequences of irresponsible acts much less shocking than 9-11, or for that matter," said Joe, "big corporation scandals, or government financial scandals. Most people can experience the consequence of pain only once before learning from that particular situation.

"For instance, a child only has to touch a hot stove and experience the shock of getting burned once to learn not to do it again. The pain becomes hard-wired as a lesson learned to avoid touching the stove in the future.

"The concern is whether or not the employees who commit financially scandalous acts will learn from the consequence of being found guilty and sentenced to pay for the crimes. How will the guilt and public sentencing influence others who are constantly exposed to temptation, and may be considering committing an illegal act? Will employees with poor ethics in the workforce serve as an example to others if they actually get fired?

"You have raised valid concerns in dealing with the principle of learning from the consequences of your actions," Joe continued. "With the shifting of society toward irresponsibility, how will the lessons learned influence future behavior? Will people take the attitude of 'I will not get caught next time,' or will they take the view that 'it was wrong to commit such an act and there will not be a next time?' If people focus on the future behavior and form the latter attitude, then this change will shift society toward a more responsible behavioral environment.

"The good news," continued Joe "is that the conditions that influence the actions regarding both large and small scale events can be changed. The fact that the negative outcome of an action occurred is proof enough that if conditions were reversed, a positive outcome will occur. Essentially what I mean is that negative breeds negative and positive breeds positive. Negative behaviors can be reversed by performing positive behaviors.

"My second principle deals with courage, pain, and pleasure. It is related to honesty.

Principle XI: Be willing to face the consequences of your actions, without letting emotional pain or pleasure compromise the truth.

Benefit: Telling the truth will set you free, regardless of what the consequences of your actions are.

"Humans are most vulnerable to acting irresponsibly when they are experiencing pain," Joe said. "For example, people can experience pain in the form of stress because they are bored at work. This is when employees are most likely to do something irresponsible. Being aware of the potential moment of weakness is important so that people can avoid doing something they may regret later."

"That's a very good principle if one has strength of character, but people like that are the minority in our society," Edward suggested.

Several of the coffee shop patrons began to nod their heads in agreement. Joe continued. "Today's society does seem to be shifting toward an environment where strong character based on morals of right or wrong is not valued as much as it once was. Currently, the blame game is more common. And more people focus on a person's outward physical appearance instead of what he or she is like inside. The good news, as I've said before, is that this can be changed.

"For example, suppose everyone in this room possesses and displays strong moral and ethical character based on doing what is right or wrong when reacting to situations in the environment. Now, imagine that this type of behavior becomes common practice every day of our lives.

"Being exposed to environments where strong character is seen all the time would have an effect on how others behave. Demonstration of strong character can be as fashionable as a person's external beauty. People have the power to shape their culture merely by establishing norms. If having a strong character were fashionable, I have no doubt that it would catch on like any other movement used to make a statement or to improve conditions," Joe concluded.

Some patrons murmured and nodded again in agreement with Joe's comments. Others sat in silence waiting for his last principle. Joe paused for a moment, surveying the expressions of the audience. Some of them were taking notes as intently as Barbara, and he sensed their eagerness to hear his last principle.

"The last principle I'm going to offer you is, in my opinion, the key ingredient to improve people's actions toward situations they face in the workplace and personal life.

Principle XII: Be positive in everything you do.

Benefits: Positive attitudes breed positive actions. Positive actions breed positive outcomes. Positive outcomes breed positive learning. Positive learning breeds positive change for future actions that create responsible behavioral environments.

"Our internal thoughts drive our reactions to situations in our environment. Internal thoughts, both conscious and unconscious, about relationships, events, work, people, and conditions are based on what we observe externally. Then we reconstruct our observations from our own perspectives. This defines our feelings, beliefs, and knowledge of the world. People are in control of their thoughts, whether or not they are aware of that power. The choice to be positive or negative, happy or unhappy, excited or bored, satisfied or unsatisfied, responsible or irresponsible is controlled by our attitudes and perceptions of the world. Remember that a positive attitude starts the chain reaction toward positive actions, consequences, learning, and environment," Joe concluded.

The coffee shop became quiet again. Then they began to applaud with approval. Joe waited, expecting a discussion to follow. This time, to his surprise, the only hand raised was Greg's who asked, "Okay, so how do we fix irresponsible behavior?"

Joe looked at his watch and said, "Come back next week and I will share with you the story of Robert who had the problem of not being responsible for his actions."

CHAPTER FIVE

Robert Joins the Workforce Environment

BEFORE THE SCHEDULED MEETING TIME, THE SERVERS WAITED FOR THE regulars to arrive. They were eager to hear the discussion that day. One of the servers, Pam, who had spoken with Joe before, was the single parent of a teenager. She had been trying, with limited success, to get her son to act more responsibly.

Joe walked in and overheard Pam saying to a co-worker, "My teenage son can be so responsible, especially when he wants something. Other times he can do things that are totally irresponsible. I tell him all the time that companies are looking for people who will act responsibly on the job."

Pam greeted Joe, and handed him his usual beverage. Joe thanked her, took a seat, and said, "I know how you feel, because I also have a teenager at home. That's why I'm going to tell you all the story of a boy who did not overcome irresponsibility until late in his career. As the saying goes, 'better late than never.'" When the other members of the group arrived shortly thereafter, they sat down with their drinks to listen to Joe's story. Pam kept an ear cocked as she chatted with customers while ringing up their purchases, eager to hear what Joe had to say about a young man he called Robert.

"Robert first entered the workforce while simultaneously attending graduate school. He worked, as part of his internship requirements, for an international manufacturing company. The internship program work experience helped build Robert an impressive résumé. Obtaining a secure job was his immediate goal. The job was important because he planned to marry his college sweetheart, Janelle, who was completing her law degree that same year.

"In the right place at the right time after graduation, Robert obtained a job as Manager of Manufacturing with a fast-growing midsize pharmaceutical company. Janelle was also on track, having secured a job at a local law firm, and the two young people were married six months later. They moved into a small apartment, and though they planned to start a family, they agreed it would be best to wait until they had worked for at least two or three years.

"While getting accustomed to married life and the workplace environment, Robert established a morning routine. He rose at six a.m. to jog for about an hour and quickly scan the world news on the Internet. His daily workload was high and tense, so while jogging, he mentally planned his work schedule in order to prioritize his management tasks. He did not have a minute to waste. He frequently worked late in the evening to respond to the high volume of e-mails and to complete other tasks.

"The fast growth of the company increased the number of tasks Robert was expected to complete, and that, in turn, increased his stress level. So, to prepare for his stressful days, after finishing his morning grooming and getting dressed, Robert performed a ritual where he stood quietly staring into the mirror for about ten minutes. He appeared to be in a trance, mesmerized by his reflection. He was meditating. Once he came out his trance, Robert raced off to face the workplace environment.

"Because of the company's rapid growth," Joe continued, "Robert was put on a fast track to the next level of management and was promoted to Director of Manufacturing after 16 months on the job.

"Robert's income increased with the promotion, and together with Janelle's income, they were able to move into a larger home in a nice middle-class neighborhood. Like so many young working couples, they were now a bit house poor, as both of their incomes were needed to maintain their new lifestyle.

"During Robert's fourth year with the company, a new position, Vice President of Operations, was created. Robert saw this as another opportunity for a promotion, but two other directors who had been with the company longer were competing for the position. The Director of Engineering had been with the company since it was founded twenty years prior. The Director of Distribution had been with the company for fifteen years. Robert had only been with the company a little over three years, but he held the advantage of being the only one of the three candidates with an MBA.

"Robert felt that he had as good a chance as the other two directors for the Operations VP promotion. Most of Robert's time in his current position was spent working with people. In school, Robert had learned that a manager's job is primarily getting work done through other people. On the job, Robert found that getting work done was based on other people's behavior, which is actually action or inaction in response to certain tasks. He knew the critical requirements needed to be successful in the VP position were interpersonal and motivational skills. In addition, he would need problem-solving skills and the ability to execute plans of action to achieve the overall goals of the company.

"During Robert's three years at the company, he had developed a democratic managerial style. His entire staff provided input in the decision making process. At the time he was fresh out of graduate school, and needed guidance from others about the best direction to take. By incorporating other people's input, he built trust, respect, and commitment.

"It's important to know that this was a company that had kept a large majority of its employees from its start twenty years prior. The founder had a no-layoff policy and a philosophy of 'those who produce will share in the profits.' The company had a generous profit-sharing program for all employees, and employee turnover was very low. Today, such long term loyalty and commitment between employer and employees are rare.

"The founder operated the company based on one common sense principle: treat others the way you want to be treated, with dignity, respect, and integrity. This principle was applied to all employees, customers, suppliers, contractors, and shareholders. It was part of the company's indoctrination of all employees, and it was understood that the principle was not to be compromised.

"When Robert joined the company, he inherited a workforce that had limited external experience, as most of the employees had not worked for any other company. Thus, their input, while valuable, had the distinct disadvantage of a narrow focus and little experience dealing with change. Their comfort level had been developed in an organization that operated like a much smaller company.

At the time Robert was competing for the Operations VP promotion, these limits were interfering with the company's ability to grow to the next performance level and compete in the international market. The international market was a new venture for the company, including Robert's staff, and luckily for Robert, he had worked for an international company during his internship in business school.

"Robert understood that the organization needed to change its culture, and the change process would require Robert to have a charismatic leadership style. Although Robert was aware that charisma was his weakness, and the company's Human Resources Department could have helped, he did not ask for assistance.

"Robert's thinking was, 'If I admit to not having charisma and needing help, others will not respect me.' Here I'll give you a little insight into Robert's background: His acute desire to be liked and respected by everyone was carried over from his childhood and teenage years. His fear of not being liked and respected influenced his decision not to seek help with his problem. He was distracted from being conscious of the origin of his hidden fear by information overload. Robert's situation is typical in many fast growing companies.

"The problem was, when put into action, some of the ideas Robert had solicited from his current staff did not advance the company's goal to support production on a global level. Instead, some ideas were implemented as window dressing. Robert cared more about being liked by others, gaining trust, and garnering respect from his staff than keeping his eye on the larger goal. He did not inform his staff that some of their less appropriate ideas would not be implemented. He often hid behind the statement 'every little bit counts' in referring to the ideas that did not advance the company goals. His fear of not being liked and respected clouded his judgment, and he therefore couldn't be honest with his staff.

"One evening," explained Joe, "an unexpected meeting occurred with one of his subordinates. Robert was working late to finish a production report and the Packaging Supervisor stopped by his office. Earl had been with the company for fifteen years, starting as a package technician and working his way up to supervisor.

"'I want to let you know how much I like working here,' Earl began, 'and I especially like being involved in the decision-making process. It makes me feel that I am valued and that the company respects me as a person, not just as a worker.'

"Earl was one of Robert's employees who had made suggestions that did not meet the company's expansion goals. Instead of being honest with Earl and sharing the truth that his idea did not meet global requirements, Robert refused to face up to his fears.

"Replying to the supervisor, Robert said, 'I'm glad you feel that way, because you have the experience to do your job better than anyone else. So, keep the ideas coming. Thanks for stopping by.'

"After the supervisor left Robert's office," Joe continued, "Robert finished his task, and in the quiet of the evening, he began to reflect on his accomplishments of the last three years. "As Robert went through his self-assessment, the reason why he was hired suddenly dawned on him. Ordinarily, the company promotes from inside, providing an inside employee was qualified for the position. When Robert was hired from outside, it was specifically because of his hands-on experience with production on an international scale. Expansion was at hand, and none of the firm's employees at that time had the necessary international experience.

He had scored an internship during graduate school with an international manufacturing company. This gave him an edge over the internal applicants. But what did Robert have to show for the company's decision to hire him three years ago? The question 'what have you done for me lately?' weighed heavily on Robert's mind. Also, he was aware that to be promoted to VP of Operations he would have to live up to the reason the company had hired him in the first place.

"Under Robert's leadership, his department had made modest improvements to support national production levels, but it was far from meeting the international production levels the company desired. This after-hours self-evaluation did not help Robert's already intense feelings of stress, and he began to worry about the performance review he faced in less than eight months. He knew that productivity would be a part of his evaluation—how could he meet the kind of goals he imagined the firm wanted for the person taking over operations? Plus he was struggling to meet his monthly house payment and needed a significant raise to live comfortably.

"One thing in particular weighed on his mind, and that was his decision to implement several ideas that had only improved production on a small scale, not coming close to the larger international demands. As he mulled over these negative issues, stress got the better of him and caused him to react impulsively."

Joe came out of his story-telling reverie and sat back in his chair. Looking around, he could see he had the attention of everyone in the coffee shop group, Pam and several of her co-workers, as well as several folks who had come upon the gathering and decided to stay.

"So?" Pam said, breaking the momentary silence, "what did he do?"

"Well, Pam," Joe replied, "Robert became obsessed with micro-managing and ultra-efficiency. Soon, he began demanding the same from his employees. He called this 'striving for excellence.' He began identifying poor performers and replacing them with what he believed to be more highly skilled workers. After six months of this style of management, the morale, trust, and respect of his employees declined. Flexibility and responsibility disappeared; working longer hours came to be an expectation. For many, the work became repetitive, task-focused, and routine. Robert expected his employees to know what to do, but did not give them proper guidelines for the job, which further worsened the behavioral environment of his department.

"Robert no longer had the positive, trusting relationship with his staff that he once had. Instead, though he was still viewed as competent, he was not well respected, trusted, or admired. Robert focused on getting the VP position, and did not notice how the shift in his approach affected the morale of his workers. His department had exceeded its production goals, so the poor morale issue remained oblivious to him. His own success was his primary goal."

Joe paused at that point and asked, "What do you think about the influence of human behavior after hearing how Robert's impulsive behavior impacted his department?"

"Boy, how situations can change so quickly," said Greg.

"Yes, and to think such rapid change can be caused by one manager's behavior," said Susan.

"It's true—sometimes we don't fully comprehend the power that we can have on the outcome of a situation," said Edward.

Joe nodded agreement, "The human behavioral factor of all organizations is the most critical factor determining success or failure of the business. And now, it looks like it is time for us all to be getting home, eh?"

"Very funny, Joe," said Pam, "My shift goes on another three hours!"

"Sorry, Pam!" Joe exclaimed, "I wouldn't want to offend such an interested listener—especially since you're the one providing me with the coffee that helps keep my chatter going." The light-hearted exchange was enough to get everyone shifting and stretching.

"So, humor me, all right?" Pam said with her hand on her hip. "What's this guy going to do about this? If I were working there, I'd be bailing pretty quick, I'll tell you that!"

"Atta girl, Pam!" exclaimed Brian. "With all this going on, what happened at Robert's performance review?"

Joe just smiled, saying, "You will just have to wait until next week when the story continues."

Joe looked at his watch as a way to bring the meeting to a close. "Obviously, there were common sense principles of responsible behavior covered earlier by this group that Robert did not apply in responding to this situation. Otherwise, the situation would have had a much different outcome. I would like everyone to think about those principles as you look into your mirror between now and next Monday. Now that you have heard this part of the story, use your reflection to identify a principle and its application and jot down what you come up with. Next week we'll go over a couple of these principles."

Joe said good night and on his way out, Pam stopped him. "Don't worry," he assured her, "I will get to the part of the story where Robert's actions as a teenager impacted him later in life.

"I'll be all ears," Pam replied.

CHAPTER SIX

The Magical Mirror

A S SOON AS EVERYONE WAS SETTLED AND QUIETED DOWN AT THE COFFEE shop the following Monday, Joe said, "I asked you to think about some of the common sense principles of responsible behavior that Robert failed to apply."

Stewart was the first to speak up. "Robert wasn't honest with himself and others. Instead, he let his fear of not being liked influence his actions. If the ideas suggested by his employees didn't contribute to the company's goal, he should have been straight with them about it. The lesson Robert needed to learn is the principle of honesty: Be honest with yourself and others in both words and actions. Principles are just words, you have to walk your talk."

"When I looked in my mirror and thought about parts of Robert's story," said Ellen, "I found that the one thing that really reached me was often when Robert was into his self-assessment, he focused on the negative aspects of his performance instead of the positive aspects. He has very hard on himself and didn't apply the principle of being positive: be positive in everything you do. If you continue to think negatively about yourself, then the negative thinking becomes a self-fulfilling prophecy.

"Some of this negative thinking caused Robert to worry excessively," she continued, "so he reacted impulsively. He failed to apply the principle of thinking about the consequence of his actions before he changed his management style to striving for excellence."

"If everyone applied the principle of considering the consequences of their actions before initiating them," said Edward, "there wouldn't be any need for 20/20 hindsight."

"There are other principles that Robert did not apply in this part of the story," said Joe, "and you have identified at least three. I want to proceed with Robert's story so we can find more of these principles and connect them with the actual behavior. Reviewing Robert's story reinforces how important it is for people to live their lives based on principles, and to have the courage to publicly stand up for them. Following these principles can prevent many of the negative consequences of people's irresponsible actions.

"Eight months after Robert began his 'striving for excellence' management approach, the time for his performance review arrived. The morning before the review Robert went through his usual routine: up at six a.m. to jog for about an hour and quickly scan the world news on the Internet. While jogging, Robert tried to prepare himself for the performance review—he visualized the process he anticipated in hopes of reducing his stress level.

"*Well, it is almost time for my performance review,*' Robert thought to himself. *'I should know the routine by now. My boss usually opens up the review with small talk, trying to show some personal concern about my well-being. I don't know how genuine his concerns are. It's probably something he learned in training about how to conduct performance reviews. After all, I have had this same training. He always starts off with good stuff about my performance. Then, the review drifts toward areas I need to work on.'*

"The constructive feedback Robert expects," said Joe, "is the classic way of identifying an employee's irresponsible actions and the need to change future actions to be more accountable.

"Robert continued his contemplations, as he thought *'I guess I will just have to grin and bear it. Maybe my boss will actually say something that is helpful. Shoot, I shouldn't worry too much because I know I have achieved and exceeded the measurable goals that my boss and I agreed upon. Of course,' Robert assured himself, 'the most important measurable goal is the bottom line of the organization, not the behavior of employees while obtaining them.*

"'Man, I'm glad I began the whole striving for excellence thing—that pushed the staff to either buy in and display some extraordinary performance—or buy out, as in bye-bye.'

"As the endorphins let loose in Robert's brain from jogging, he assured himself further. *'I believe that most employees can and want to do more. So, how can anyone not want to strive for excellence? The department production figures are very good, which supports the view that I made a good decision. This might be just what I need to give me a chance for the VP promotion.'*

"After Robert finished his morning grooming and got dressed, he again performed his ritual of staring into the mirror for about ten minutes before going to work.

The Performance Review

"Robert met with his supervisor in the afternoon to discuss his performance. Robert's production figures were 15 percent above goal, but in the past six months, production had been shifting downward. The absentee rate of Robert's employees' had climbed. What got his supervisor's attention was that his employee turnover rate, which had been zero for over two years, was now up by 1 percent. While this was still lower than the industry's average of 3 percent, several workers had been complaining about the atmosphere in Robert's department. Robert was not aware of any complaints."

"As Robert expected," continued Joe, "his supervisor began the discussion with small talk and asked how his family was doing. Robert and his wife were involved with the local community Boys and Girls Clubs, a company sponsored project, and they chatted a bit about that. After this went on for a while, Robert began to show some signs of impatience. He wanted to get on with his performance review.

"His supervisor noticed Robert's impatience, so he shifted in his seat and signaled with his body language that the performance review was starting. He began, as expected, on a positive note. 'In reviewing your production figures, I see that you are doing very well,' he said. 'They are running above the goals we agreed upon. To be exact, your department has exceeded your goal by 15 percent. In addition, your department managed to achieve these goals while maintaining an operating budget under 10 percent. Keep up the good work.'

"'Thanks,' Robert said. 'I will pass your comments on to my department. They are striving for excellence.'

"At that point in the discussion," Joe said, "there was a silence between the two.

"'How is the striving for excellence concept working for your department overall?' Robert's supervisor asked.

"Robert was a little surprised by this question since that specific management concept was emphasized in many management books by expert consultants. 'It's going very well,' Robert replied. 'Production figures are 15 percent above goal and the budget is 10 percent under goal, as you mentioned earlier.'

"Robert was curious as to why his boss was asking the question," Joe said. "He asked himself, *'Why would anyone not want to strive for excellence? Don't the production results speak for themselves?'*

"'The reason I asked about the excellence approach is that while your production figures are still well above goals, they have been trending downward for the last six months. At the same time, employee turnover and absenteeism are going up,' said Robert's supervisor.

"'That is one good thing about the excellence approach,' Robert said. 'People can do more, and most want to do more. There were a few employees who couldn't carry their weight, but then they shouldn't have been a part of the team anyway.'

"'What about those who want to do more, but get overwhelmed with work to the point where they have lost balance in their lives?' Robert's supervisor asked. 'These workers become burned out by the demands of excellence because their work has now become routine and boring. These workers will also leave the company, even if they wanted to do more.'

"'I hadn't thought of it that way,' Robert said, starting to feel uncomfortable. 'Has anyone complained about being overworked?'

"'Not to me directly, but I suggest that you talk to the Human Resources Manager. I understand there have been complaints. The workers wanted to keep it confidential for fear of retribution or being fired,' Robert's supervisor replied.

"Robert was surprised to hear this. He hadn't realized that anyone on his team was unhappy. However, as he reflected on the department over the past six months, he realized that his focus was more on how his management style could help him get the VP position, not on workers' contentment with their jobs.

"'Robert,' his supervisor said, 'your first three years' performance was outstanding. Trust, commitment, and morale were high. Absenteeism and turnover rates were low. Now, don't misunderstand me, there is nothing wrong with expecting more from your employees. Goals should be challenging and should broaden the employees' horizons as long as the goals are realistic.

'The more demanding approach should be a win/win situation for both the company and the employees with a proper system of motivations and rewards. On the other hand, being obsessed with excellence can be a turnoff. I know, because I made that mistake early in my management career,' the supervisor concluded.

"Robert felt bad. At the same time," Joe clarified, "he respected his boss for his honesty. Robert left the meeting thinking that he would need to make some changes if he were going to have a chance at the VP position."

Joe stopped briefly at this point to get feedback from the listeners. "So, let's take a few minutes to talk about the principles applied in Robert's performance review."

"Robert's boss applied the principle of honesty by giving feedback on the striving for excellence approach," pointed out Brian. "He also applied the principle of admitting to his past mistakes in using the excellence management style. Robert seemed surprised that this style had a downside. He came away from the review respecting his boss for sharing it with him."

"On the other hand," said Edward, "Robert was so wrapped up in pursuing the VP position that he failed to apply the principle of pursuing your own well being while respecting the needs of others. Some of his employees needed a more balanced life, while others needed flexibility in job assignments. This was apparent when his turnover rate went up."

Who Do You See in the Mirror?

Joe continued. "All right," he said, smiling. "You're on the ball with these principles! Let's see if Robert got it. The next morning as Robert finished going through his normal routine of jogging and grooming, he found himself staring into the mirror as usual. Then, a strange thing happened. He heard a voice asking, 'Who do you see in the mirror?'

"Robert looked around to see if his wife had just walked into the bathroom. There was no one there. The voice came again. 'Who do you see in the mirror?'

"This time, Robert decided to go along with whoever was playing a trick on him, so he responded to the question, saying, 'I see myself in the mirror.'

"Then the voice asked, 'Why do you stare into the mirror after you have finished grooming and checking your physical appearance each morning?'

"'I'm preparing myself mentally to face what I know will be a challenging and difficult work day. I find I often behave differently in similar situations and don't know why I inconsistently change my behavior. I am trying to figure myself out.'

"'Would you like to know why you behave the way you do? Much can be revealed through a human behavior makeover. Are you interested?' the Magical Mirror asked.

"'Well. Okay,' Robert said a little apprehensively. He had never heard a mirror talk before. 'What am I supposed to do and when do I begin?'

"'Starting today' the Mirror said. 'you will have one assignment each day. You are to write down notes of your activities. As you go through your daily tasks, record your feelings, thoughts, actions, and inactions as you respond to situations. We will meet every morning at this same time to proceed with the human behavior makeover. This will be as easy as hooking up your television cable box.'

"Robert decided whatever was going on here was good for him, and was probably just his own learning coming up from his unconsciousness. Or something like that. He decided not to try to figure it out, but rather just dive in—he hadn't liked his performance review, he was nervous about his chances for getting the VP position and he was ready for change—even if it was coming from a talking mirror. *'Hey,'* he thought, *'either I'm cracking up or I'm onto something—either way, I'll give it a try.'*

"That day there was a meeting concerning a backorder problem with one of the company's best-selling products. Robert's department Packaging Manager had called the meeting. Also attending were the Purchasing Manager, who was responsible for buying a part for one of the packaging machines, and the Human Resources Manager, who was responsible for supplying workers to operate the packaging machines.

"Robert called the meeting to order. He asked the Packaging Manager to define the problem and give an update.

"'The packaging machine is down because of a broken part,' the Packaging Manager explained. 'The broken part has been ordered, but it has to be fabricated. Normally, it would take two weeks to get the part, but I pressured the supplier to work overtime, so we'll have the part in six days. Meanwhile, we'll need 5,000 units just to catch up with the backorders and keep up with our regular monthly orders.'

"'How did the problem get this big before we were aware of it?' Robert asked the group. There was silence.

"The Packaging Manager finally spoke up. 'About two and a half weeks ago, I learned about the need for the part, and the two-week lead-time on the part. That was when I held a meeting with Purchasing to resolve the issue. Later I briefed Human Resources in anticipation of a possible need for extra support staff.'

"Robert asked the Purchasing Manager when the Maintenance Department had told him about needing the part. The Purchasing Manager replied, 'Two weeks ago.'

"Robert saw where this conversation was going, and asked, 'What other options are available to help us resolve this problem?'

"The Purchasing Manager, who was also responsible for outside contract manufacturing, said, 'We have exhausted our options of getting help from outside contractors. Our only other option becomes available once the machine part is express shipped to us. Then we could go to a three-shift operation and catch up with the backorders within two weeks. We've got enough materials in inventory to support a three-shift level.'

"At that point in the discussion, Robert remembered a Planning and Scheduling meeting two months earlier that addressed the increased demand for the product. Robert's Packaging Manager was not part of that meeting. During that meeting, it had been decided that action should be taken to increase production to meet greater demand. Gearing up production had been delegated to Robert, who thought he had passed that information on to his Packaging Manager, but he had forgotten to do so. If he had passed on that information, this whole problem could have been avoided. Standard operating procedures called for ordering additional machine parts when production increased by double its current levels.

"'It sounds like the group has a plan to catch up with the back order situation by going to a three-shift operation,' Robert said. 'Let's implement the plan, and keep me informed of the status.'

"Robert's stomach felt a little queasy as he concluded the meeting. The Planning and Scheduling meeting he had attended was on his conscience, but he took no action. Meanwhile, Robert's Packaging Manager left the meeting feeling responsible for dropping the ball by not taking action soon enough after the meetings with Purchasing and Human Resources.

"The next morning as Robert began his day, he wondered if the Magical Mirror would show up. He felt excited and curious about what the Magical Mirror had in store for him and hoped it would come again. He hurried through his morning routine, wondering about the makeover. *'Will the mirror be able to show my character traits? If so, what will they look like? Or, will my physical characteristics change?'* Robert thought this over while jogging. He didn't have the slightest idea what to expect.

"When it came time to stare into the mirror, Robert thought that his appearance in the mirror was just the same as it was the day before, except that he had different clothes on.

"The Magical Mirror did show up and asked Robert 'Who do you see in the mirror?'

"Robert responded, 'I see myself.' He was still unable to make the connection between his daily tasks and his feelings, thoughts, and actions.

"'What did you feel, think, and do when you met with the Packaging, Purchasing, and Human Resources Managers to discuss the production down time and back order problem?' the Mirror asked.

"'I was frustrated and wondered how we could have avoided the problem. I had hoped to learn from the experience for future reference,' Robert replied.

"Robert was still unwilling to admit to his own inaction, using 'we' instead of 'I' when referring to how the problem could have been avoided. Perhaps he was just playing the blame game. Robert's failure to communicate the need to gear up production to his Packaging Manager, as discussed in the Planning and Scheduling meeting, prevented other employees from taking action. Others could have taken steps to remedy the situation before the machine shut down. Robert did not intentionally withhold this information from Packaging. Instead, he was simply overwhelmed with too much work that day, and that task fell through the cracks.

"Instead of admitting to an entirely human, forgivable mistake, Robert lacked the courage to face the consequences of his inaction," Joe explained. "Sooner or later, someone will realize that Robert was indeed present at the Planning and Scheduling meeting, and that he failed to pass the information on. In his current state of mind, afraid of making the slightest mistake, he was willing to take the risk of remaining silent."

Joe paused, glancing at the coffee shop audience. He had reached a point in the story where he wanted to involve the patrons in the observation of Robert's actions. He stated, "There are some principles of responsibility that, if applied, could have helped Robert avoid the consequences of his inactions. What are some of those principles that you can identify before I continue the story?"

"The honesty principle is all over this story," Brian said. "The lesson that Robert should have gained from this experience is that telling the truth is always the best policy. It will set you free from self-recrimination."

"Admit your mistakes; it is better to lose face than try to save face on false pretenses," added Susan. "The other lesson that Robert should have gained from this experience is that humans are not perfect."

"Robert's mistake was not intentional," said Ellen. "But, once he realized his mistake, he applied the principles, didn't he? He took full ownership for his inaction and learned from the consequence of that inaction."

Barbara spoke up quickly, "No. Robert didn't take ownership. He didn't go with the principle about having the courage to do the right thing, especially when confronted with a difficult situation that challenges your strength of character. He gave in to his fears, and was embarrassed for making the mistake."

"There are many people who feel mistakes are a sign of weakness," Joe added, "but in actuality, mistakes can be a sign of strength as long as you apply the principle of learning from the consequences. The principle must also become part of the person's character."

Current Behavior and Past Behavior Connection

Joe continued his story about Robert. "'How did you feel when you realized you forgot to pass on the Planning and Scheduling information?' the Mirror asked.

"'At first, I felt frustrated with myself and embarrassed about making the mistake,' Robert said. 'Then, I worried about losing my employees' respect for making such an obvious error.'

"'After your initial emotional reactions, how did you deal with the situation caused by your mistake?' asked the mirror.

"'Well, I tried to understand how I could have done that,' said Robert. 'I wanted to tell the Packaging, Purchasing, and Human Resources Managers that I had made a mistake, but I just couldn't. Then, I justified my silence by telling myself that it was simply water under the bridge. The situation couldn't be changed, but I could learn from it for the future.'

"'Can you remember at least one incident during your childhood when you felt that way?' asked the Magical Mirror.

"A memory slowly rose to the surface of his consciousness. 'Yes,' said Robert quietly. 'When I was twelve, I decided to cut class with my friends. I enjoyed being with them, and I always had a lot of fun with them.'

"'Even though it was my first time cutting class, and I knew it was wrong, I did it anyway. I wanted my friends to like me and accept me as one of them. But afterwards, I was the only one who was punished by the teacher for cutting class. The next day, the teacher asked me why I wasn't in class—in front of all the other students. I felt really embarrassed and after school, my friends teased me. I got caught and the others didn't. They held it over me for ages.'

"'Can you describe the behavioral environment in your classroom?' asked the Magical Mirror.

"'Some days, kids would cut classes, and were not punished by the teacher,' Robert recalled. 'But other times, kids caught cutting class would be punished. The rule for cutting class was applied inconsistently, and some kids got away with it while others didn't,' explained Robert.

"'Can you remember another situation where you felt confused about what the correct behavior was?' asked the Magical Mirror.

"'Yes,' said Robert. 'When I was 16, I hung out at the mall with my friends after school. I loved hanging out with them and going to parties. One of my close friends had a car and driver's license. He wasn't even required to have an adult in the car with him. So, four of us went with him to a party. The guy driving drank alcohol at the party.

"'I made the mistake of going with them; I wanted to be with my friends. Besides, they would have called me a chicken for not going. They probably wouldn't have accepted me as one of the group, either. There was a car accident. I was the lucky one. I only got hurt a little. My friends weren't so lucky. They sustained some pretty serious injuries—two of the guys had injuries that were life threatening. My parents were very upset with my irresponsible actions, to say the least. I felt so bad that I had made such a stupid mistake.'"

"'What type of family environment did you grow up in?' the Mirror asked.

"'There are four in our family: my mother, my father, me, and my younger sister,' replied Robert. 'We lived in a middle class neighborhood. Both of my parents worked hard to provide shelter, food, clothes, education, transportation, and entertainment for us.

"'During my early childhood, life was pretty structured, but the rules were sometimes inconsistent and confusing. For example, Mom usually took the lead in enforcing the rules, like monitoring TV programs, making sure homework got done, providing proper nutrition, assigning chores, modeling moral values, and so on.

"'My father was present, but he didn't speak up as much as my mother did when enforcing the rules. One example of the confusing rules is when we would go out to eat. My mother would always remind me that it was not good behavior to leave my baseball cap on while we ate. Yet, my father kept his cap on even when we ate out. Always. I remember looking at him across the table, so very cool in his cap, while I was feeling that I looked ordinary just like any other kid with my bare head. It doesn't seem like much, but it stuck with me.

"'I noticed another inconsistency when I was old enough to drive,' continued Robert. 'My father taught me to follow the speed limit, leave enough space between cars, and fasten my seat belt. Yet, most of the time he didn't follow those rules when he drove. On the other hand, my mother always followed the driving rules. I knew what was right but could not figure out when to do it right and when not to do it the right way. It was very confusing.'

"'If you had to sum up your childhood years, what words would you use to express your feelings?' the Mirror asked.

"'Basically happy but also confused, unstable, and frustrated. But I always felt happy when I was with my friends,' Robert answered.

"'Can you describe what made you happier when you were with your friends?' the Mirror asked.

"'A sense of belonging, acceptance, understanding, and identification. They were growing up in the same kind of environment that I was in. I could relate to them,' replied Robert. 'Is there a connection between my past behavior and my behavior now? Some of these incidents happened more than fifteen years ago.'

"'Absolutely,' replied the Magical Mirror. 'Some people are aware of such a connection, but for others to make the connection requires them to return to the basic building blocks of the human behavior process. This can be accomplished by the behavioral makeover I mentioned. It's like a complete re-education, such as relearning the alphabet, but much easier. There are 26 letters of the alphabet to remember, but only five elements that make up the human behavior process.'

"Robert pondered this for a moment. 'It sounds intriguing. Tell me about these five elements.'"

CHAPTER SEVEN

The Five Elements of the
Human Behavior Process

"THE MIRROR DIMMED TO A PALE HAZE. AS ROBERT LOOKED ON, FIVE letters materialized and floated upon its cloudy surface. The mirror spoke and began to explain their meanings.

"'The five elements of the human behavior process are *Consequence, Attitude, Behavior, Learning,* and *Environment.* If you put together the first letters of those five words, they spell the word CABLE, and together, the five processes make up what we'll call the HUMAN *CABLE SYSTEM.*'

"Robert was listening carefully, and without realizing it, repeated what the mirror had said, 'HUMAN CABLE SYSTEM, hmmm.'

"'Yes,' confirmed the mirror. 'We can just call it the HCS for now. It's an innovative way of looking at human behavior. It's holistic—it considers both learned and natural reactions in the responses people have to the situations that make up their lives." The floating letters in the mirror lined up to form the word CABLE.

"'Awareness of the HUMAN CABLE SYSTEM will give you tools to help you improve your behavior in ways that could very likely make your life better. The way you behave has been, shall we say, wired in your mind from past experiences,' said the voice within the mirror.

"'What motivates you humans to behave the way you do is your natural instinct to satisfy your physical, security, stability, psychological and social needs. In every situation, the results of your behavior work either toward satisfying those needs or not—and that's what wires your behavior for the next time that situation arises.

"'A classic example is how a young child, attempting to satisfy its curiosity, touches a hot stove for the first time and gets burned. The consequence of being burned by the hot stove wires the child's HCS not to touch the stove again.'

"Though bearing no semblance of a face, the mirror seemed to stare through Robert, as if summoning his true intentions. 'However,' the voice continued, 'this is an arduous, involved process. Like any change, it will not happen overnight. A *desire* to change is absolutely essential, and finding that desire can be the highest hill to climb. You need to have the willpower to change. Once you commit the desire and willpower, the process will require effort, focus, courage, and perseverance. Robert, do you truly want to change?'

"'Yes,' Robert said, thinking about the possible promotion. 'How do I start? There are five elements in the HUMAN CABLE SYSTEM— do I take them one at a time and in order? Are there exercises or assignments?' He was excited about this opportunity to become a more satisfied and successful person, but it was a lot to take in. For starters, his mirror was talking to him. How weird! But he just had to accept that this was meant to be and try to organize his thinking.

"'All of the CABLE elements are important as a group, but I do like to jumble the letters up a bit. The process has best served others in your predicament by starting with **B** – Behavior, **L** – Learning, and **C** – Consequence. Behavior is simply everything that humans do or fail to do when responding to their environment. Behavior is important to focus on early in your quest to change, because without action and inaction, and your associated behavioral reaction, there are no consequences. Learning and Consequences are naturally high up in the elements of the system. If nothing is learned from experiencing the consequence of an action or inaction, nothing is gained toward more responsible behavior.'

"'If a person takes no action in a situation, how can there be consequences?' Robert asked.

"'An example of inaction occurred in the production meeting when you chose not to tell the Packaging, Purchasing, and Human Resources Managers the possible repercussions of ramping up production,' replied the mirror. 'Your inaction indirectly resulted in the lack of having enough spare parts on hand in case the packaging machine broke down. The consequence also caused emotional pain for your Packaging Manager because he thought he was at fault for not doing enough to prevent the machine from going down.'

"'I see,' Robert said. 'I feel awful about that. I don't want to let it happen again. What about my attitude?' he asked. 'Where does that fit in the whole scheme of the Human CABLE System?'

"'The Attitude element refers to whether a person responds positively or negatively in a given situation,' the mirror replied. 'For example, imagine a worker—we'll call this worker Tom—in a behavioral environment where a large number of fellow employees are bored. They deal with their boredom by constantly speaking negatively about the job and blaming their co-workers and management. As Tom interacts with these bored, listless co-workers, he internalizes his experience. He reconstructs the situation in his own frame of reference about his workplace, and as a result, Tom finds that negativity also becomes his Attitude toward the job.'

"'I think I get it,' Robert said. 'You're saying behavior is a result of attitude.'

"'Correct,' the Magical Mirror replied. 'Workers in any sort of organization will speak either favorably or unfavorably about their jobs, and some employees will simply do nothing. Once an employee decides to respond to coworkers, management, or the job as a whole, based on his or her own internal reaction, that employee outwardly behaves in ways that may well result in a consequence.

"'For example, let's say a group of employees decide not to complete a task because they find the task boring or beneath them. The employees' decision to not complete the task is an outward behavior that is an observable element in the workplace environment. The repercussions of not completing the task could be a reprimand,

88

counseling, or even termination. Whether the consequence provides pleasure or pain determines the frequency of the action. If the employees experienced not completing the task as a pleasure that relieved their boredom, they may repeat that behavior. On the other hand, if not completing the task resulted in the employees being disciplined in some way, they may choose not to repeat the behavior.'

"Robert realized it had been his desire for social acceptance that had caused him to compromise his own responsible behavior. He was surprised to grasp that he had always wanted to be liked by his friends. The memory of that car accident when he was 16 loomed. He knew if he thought about it long enough, he would be able to list far too many situations where his need to be liked and accepted had marred his judgment and led him to ignore his core value of being responsible. Robert's face became brighter as he stared into the mirror. Then he gave a sigh of relief as if the weight of years of mistakes were suddenly lifted from his body. The letters in the mirror disappeared, leaving only the image of a man intoxicated by new ideas.

"'I must go now,'" said the Magical Mirror, 'but before I leave, I must ask, who do you see in the mirror?'

"'I still see myself in the mirror,' Robert said, 'but my image is much clearer now. I feel that I'm no longer blinded by the reflection of my own self-centered needs. I've become aware of my desire to be liked by all at the cost of being honest with myself and others. This awareness is uplifting.'

"Robert went back to his office that day with a new and improved attitude. He still wanted that VP promotion, but he now knew he had to make some behavioral changes to earn it."

Joe sat back in his seat. As he had been telling the story, he had not realized that he had captured the attention of everyone in the coffee shop that evening. When the applause came, he was startled at first, but then grinned widely.

"Come back and listen next week," he said. "I'll tell you the story of someone who was a little bit too responsible, and how she was able to get back in balance."

CHAPTER EIGHT

Donna Joins the
Workforce Environment

DURING THE WEEK, THE REGULAR COFFEE SHOP PATRONS TOLD THEIR friends about the meetings that took place, the stories they had heard, and the lessons they had learned. Robert's story illustrated to them that it just might be possible to change irresponsible behavior using a common sense behavioral makeover.

The people who had heard Joe tell Robert's story were buzzing about the ideas in the Magical Mirror's HUMAN CABLE SYSTEM. As Monday approached, many of the regulars found themselves trying to explain HCS to their friends and relatives. Several invited others to join them to hear Joe's next story about someone whose behavior was the opposite of Robert's.

Reflecting on the previous week's discussion, the group's attention was focused on Joe's idea of the behavioral makeover. Most had heard about extreme makeovers to alter a person's physical appearance or their home, but they had never heard about a "rewiring" makeover process for altering irresponsible behavior. They were intrigued to hear more about the HUMAN CABLE SYSTEM rewiring makeover concept, used as a tool to alter people's behavior.

When Joe and the regulars showed up for the next meeting, they were greeted by a crowd of expectant new faces. In the crowd, Joe noticed many young people and he was glad to see them. The servers were busier than ever taking care of everyone. They were happy to have the increased business, but at the same time, they weren't happy that they could not listen closely to the group's discussion. The patrons took their seats, got their drinks, and then Joe faced the group to tell his new story. But before he could begin, Greg stood up and requested time for a short discussion about Robert's tale.

"Could HCS really have an impact in shifting society toward a responsible world?" Greg asked. "Isn't irresponsible behavior a part of life which society seems to accept?

"Yeah," Brian commented, "Sometimes I think society as a whole has become immune to this shift toward irresponsibility we've been talking about. I'm not so sure any one person can start a trend that will change our whole society."

"I have my doubts, too," Ellen said. "If each person continues to stand by and watch, then our society will continue the negative shift."

"Well, I respectfully have to disagree with you three," Barbara announced. "I'm certainly not willing to sit idly by and let society continue to roll downhill. I'm ready to take action to stop it. Let's not forget Joe's challenge that each person can act to become part of a movement of responsibility. Movements work—if enough people are committed to this, I believe it could indeed reverse irresponsible behavior in our culture. You just have to start with the person you see in the mirror."

"Look," Edward said thoughtfully, "Reversing the trend is basically a common sense approach that only requires you to study your own behavior. There have been so many studies and so much research about human behavior, I worry that people actually learning to behave differently gets lost in the shuffle. I think it's a matter of thinking outside the box—thinking about things differently."

"Welcome everyone!" Joe managed to say amidst the chatter these comments had stirred up. "It's very gratifying to find you exploring the ideas I've presented to you. I wholeheartedly agree it's beneficial to look at what we've learned so far. Edward, you are certainly right about thinking outside the box. This new thinking requires using common sense responsible principles experienced in real life situations, not empirically controlled studies. These studies are definitely valuable, but they frequently over analyze the situation. The Magical Mirror in the story of Robert asks that we be aware of the five elements that make up human behavior.

"Let me go over them once more for the new folks who have joined us. We've been focusing on a system I call the HUMAN CABLE SYSTEM™. CABLE stands for Consequences, Attitude, Behavior, Learning, and Environment. These five elements are involved in determining how people behave.

"I've brought along a few illustrations that depict how the five elements are connected—or sometimes disconnected. Susan, could you please start passing these copies around the room?" Joe asked, handing her the papers. "The cause/effect connection is explained as follows:

"People's negative or positive attitudes toward a situation, represented by an A+ or an A- for Attitude, cause them to behave—the B+ or B- for Behavior in the diagram—in a negative or positive manner. When people behave, it always results in a negative or positive consequence—that's the C+ and C- for Consequence—from which to learn and change future behavior. Thus, there is always a negative or positive learning experienced—L+ or L- for Learning. The negative or positive learning experience becomes part of the future behavioral environment for people to model and influence others—thus, the E+ or E- for Environment in the diagram."

The room grew quiet except for the sounds of the papers being passed, and Joe waited for people to get the illustration and have a chance to look at it for a few moments.

When Joe saw the audience's eyes upon him once more, he continued. "This new concept is simple, but radically different from the current cultural mindset that treats the five elements of the human behavior system (HBS) as disconnected entities. The HCS treats all five elements in a holistic manner. All of the elements are interconnected as depicted in the HCS illustration."

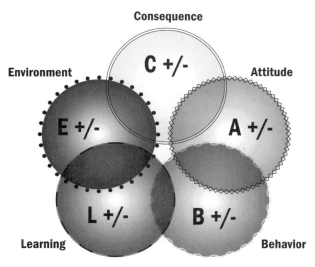

Human CABLE System™ (HCS)

"A real life example of a person exhibiting responsible behavior that closely exemplifies the HCS illustration is the CEO of Japan Airlines. The CEO, who was responsible for successfully managing Japan Airlines during some tough economic times, used a 'lead by example' approach to achieve his goals. As discussed previously, the CEO rides a public bus to work. He reduced his salary to about $90,000 a year when he had to ask his employees to accept reduced salaries. He removed the walls of his office so he could literally have an open door atmosphere and be available to all his employees. His actions matched his words. Another example of actions matching a CEO's words is a situation with Miami banker Leonard Abess Jr. He sold his majority stake in City National Bancshares and out of his own pocket gave $60 million of the proceeds to his employees. The gifted employees included tellers, bookkeepers, clerks, etc., all 399 workers on his payroll and 72 retired former employees. In contrast, as America and the rest of the world face the worst economic crisis since the great depression, there are other CEOs of major corporations that on the surface appeared to reduce their salaries by only accepting one dollar a year but they simultaneously accepted hefty compensation in stocks and/or bonuses. But the good news is there were 15 of the top AIG executives who returned their entire bonus money after politicians and taxpayers voiced their outrage by this irresponsible act. Still, it does not negate the fact that some banks, mortgage companies, automotive manufacturing plants, investment banks, and insurance corporations actually did pay their CEOs only one dollar a year. These companies and their CEOs acted responsibly."

Joe paused for a few moments to let the group fully digest what he had been explaining. When they were ready he began talking about the next illustration in his handouts. "In contrast to the HCS illustration, the HBS illustration depicts the disconnected mind-set of the five human behavioral elements; attitude, behavior, consequence, learning, and environment." He started by citing some typical examples of irresponsible behavior associated with disconnected mindset thinking.

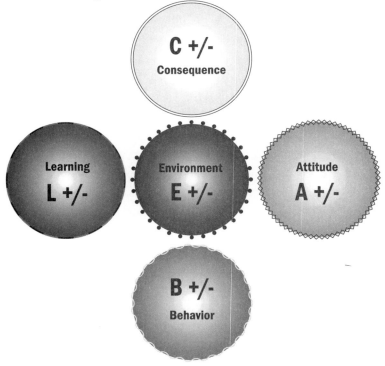

Human Behavioral System (HBS)

"Employees who steal money or office supplies from their employer do not think about the consequences of their actions; like getting caught and being held accountable. Often, they are not thinking at all. They take certain actions for granted and do not realize the actions are unacceptable or illegal. Yet, despite the negative consequences of possible termination and/or legal penalties, some employees still commit these acts on a regular basis. This type of behavior clearly shows a disconnection between the attitude, behavior, learning, and consequence elements. Usually, a person with this mindset will be influenced by the same behavior pattern modeled by other people in their work environment.

"As described earlier in our discussion, examples of irresponsible behavior linked to the economic crisis exhibit some of the same behavioral element disconnection. The economic crisis revealed serious irresponsible acts such as the out of control spending in corporate America. This included outlandish compensation for senior management personnel in many companies, the purchase and use of unnecessary lavish private jets, and over-the-top expensive office redecoration. These irresponsible acts were done at a time when senior management of these same companies was asking American taxpayers for money to help keep their companies from failing.

"Likewise, at a lower level, many consumers were living way above their means. They got caught with housing loans they could not repay. The alleged ponzi securities fraud scheme, the Illinois governor's impeachment, and multiple government official sex scandals are other examples of this commonly occurring irresponsible behavior.

"The stereotypical behavior displayed by many members of the House of Representatives and the Senate is often driven more by self interest, instead of by what is right for the country and the needs of the American people. This behavior also falls under the category of an irresponsible act."

"The mindset of the status quo has consistently resulted in a short-term rollercoaster behavioral pattern for years. An on-again-off-again relationship between two people is a prime example of a roller-coaster behavioral pattern. This type of relationship usually requires a sustainable change in behavior from one or both people to make the relationship work. Often, the agreed upon modified behavior ends up lasting for only a short time before a person reverts to his or her previous behavior. Breaking out of this mode of behavior is the challenge we face.

"I hope that makes the concept of CABLE more understandable," Joe said. "Are you ready to move on now to another story that illustrates these ideas?" Much nodding and murmurs of assent followed.

"Good, thanks. Last week, we saw how Robert began to overcome irresponsible behavior by using the HUMAN CABLE SYSTEM rewiring makeover process. Just as the avoidance of responsibility in everyday life can cause some serious consequences, the opposite can be just as damaging. Today, I'm going to tell the story of a young woman who was overly responsible. People took advantage of her because she was too ready to take the blame. Perhaps you know someone who behaves like this in the workplace or in your personal life.

"There are three parts to the story that I will share with you. First, Donna faces the workplace behavioral environment situation. Second, Donna searches for a link between her upbringing and workplace behavioral environment. Third, she seeks help from the Magical Mirror to deal with her doubts about responsible behavior.

"The story begins with Donna entering the workforce after her graduation from college with a Bachelor of Science in textile chemistry and a minor in business. She obtained a position at a textile think-tank organization. She had been with the company for only a year and a half before her boss noticed her exceptional leadership skills and promoted her to Project Manager. Her job included supervising the tasks and activities of five research assistants she referred to as team members. In addition to her immediate staff responsibilities, she also worked with four other Project Managers.

"Donna used a management style in which she, as leader, gave constructive feedback to her team members. She was not the kind of leader who never admitted to being wrong. Instead, she consistently took responsibility for her own actions. She set high standards for success—for both herself and the team members who worked with her. She gave her staff the freedom to innovate, experiment, and take risks without fear of reprimand. She gave challenging assignments and was willing to put up with short-term failures to learn from long-term gains.

"After Donna had been Project Manager for about a year, she ran into trouble when her team's research project did not meet its deadline for a new fiber to be submitted to the Federal Trade Commission for approval. The application to the FTC was delayed by six months, which resulted in a loss of potential profits due to postponing the sales and marketing campaign.

"Donna called a team meeting to discuss the delay. During the meeting, each of her team members blamed others to explain why the project was late. No one wanted to admit that he or she had any part in the delay. Donna knew that this type of finger-pointing only created a defensive atmosphere that would distract from getting the team to focus on resolving the problem. Instead of letting the meeting continue with the distraction, she defused the blame game her team members and co-workers were playing. She relied on the past 'wiring' of her behavior—a subconscious response of which she was not consciously aware, and took all the blame, thinking that as Project Manager, she should have made sure everyone else was doing their tasks to meet the project deadline.

"Donna did not micromanage each and every task. Micromanagement, from Donna's perspective, indicated a lack of confidence in her employees' abilities and a lack of trust in the team. Instead of micromanaging, she regularly reviewed the project's goals and objectives with the team. In addition, she explained how each team member's individual tasks fit within the overall goal. Accepting their performance expectations, Donna created task assignments for each team member based on his or her abilities and desire to perform. She respected and trusted employees to be responsible for their own actions and inactions in performing their tasks.

"However, reality set in when her department's goal was not achieved. Donna's team members were only too happy to agree that she should be responsible and take the blame for the outcome. Her co-workers were also relieved when Donna took responsibility for the project delay. After all, her team's members and co-workers would be relieved of having to take responsibility for their part in missing the deadline. On the other hand, when the goals of other projects were achieved, the team members were happy to share in taking credit for their success.

"'As project leader, I am responsible for the project missing its target date,' Donna said. 'Having said that, at our next meeting, I want each of you to focus on both what the team did right, and what the team needs to improve on so we can learn from the consequence of missing the target date. I suggest that you all re-examine our communication, coordination, and follow-up systems. We must keep this problem from happening again.'

"Donna's team members and co-workers left the meeting feeling they had not dropped the ball, but this was not the first time Donna had taken responsibility for problems. She had a reputation of being a highly responsible person, perhaps too responsible. She often took responsibility whether she directly or indirectly contributed to causing a problem. Donna felt that taking responsibility for negative outcomes of projects would allow her team to focus on resolving the problem without letting their personal blame prevent them from finding a solution.

"Donna's action to take total responsibility for the negative outcome—the consequence—became part of the staff's behavioral environment. Her actions had an effect on the team members' actions. For example, each team member observed Donna's actions, and then reconstructed her actions from their own perspective. Then, each team member responded to Donna's choice of taking total responsibility for the outcome. I refer to this as the 'influence factor.'

"The team could have responded in a couple of ways. A team member could admit to his or her role in contributing to the problem, or blame other members of the team. A final option was to let Donna take full responsibility. Each team member's response to Donna's actions depended on his or her character.

"Let me point out, though, that the weakness in Donna's approach is that it did not allow her team to be responsible for their own actions or inactions. Her team knew that after Donna had taken total responsibility, she would only give them constructive feedback for their contributions. Donna, on the other hand, thought that her team members were beginning to take advantage of her responsible response to problems. She wanted to lead by setting an example of responsible behavior and hoped that her employees would follow her example. Instead, her employees reacted by blaming other team members and began to slack off. They knew they would not be held accountable, so their work habits began to be more careless and more errors were being made.

"Donna went back to her office after the team meeting feeling somewhat frustrated with the outcome and how irresponsibly the team behaved. This type of irresponsible behavior seemed to fall into a pattern. She sat in her office in the quiet of the evening trying to make sense of what was happening. Donna was not consciously aware of why she took excessive responsibility for her actions most of the time. Acting responsibly had been normal behavior for her since childhood. She could not understand why anyone would act differently. Yet, an increasing number of people who crossed her path seemed to think that blaming others was a way to survive in today's environment. Thus, she started to have doubts about always being responsible for her actions. She was confused.

"Donna realized she had a need to figure out if it was always appropriate to take the blame for employee problems, and if not, what she could do instead." Joe paused. "Okay, folks, what do you think Donna should do?" People murmured and began raising their hands.

"No, take some time to think it over," Joe said. "Come back next week to hear how Donna searched for the root cause of why she always behaved overly responsibly."

Some of the regulars stayed around the coffee shop after Joe paid his bill and said his goodbyes to the group. Edward said, "I can relate to the situation that Donna is faced with. I work in a non-union shop environment. At my garage, when an employee has the courage to take responsibility for problems, the others who contributed to the problems just sit by and let him or her take the blame. For instance, in Donna's situation, she is the project leader, and has overall responsibility for the project. But each of her team members also has the responsibility for their individual tasks necessary to meet their deadline. So, in my mind, the team shares responsibility for achieving the desired outcome. Donna, on the other hand, must hold each team member accountable for their part."

Stewart spoke next. "I work in a management versus non-management adversarial behavioral environment where sharing responsibilities as a team, like in Donna's situation, is a real challenge. A union represents the non-management labor workforce. There are two main ingredients needed to have shared responsibilities working as a team in my company. The first ingredient is trust, and the second is having common performance goals for success that can be measured and recognized by both parties.

"Unfortunately, in an adversarial relationship like the one I'm in" Stewart continued, "trust is often non-existent between management and the labor union. The lack of trust causes a ripple effect throughout the entire organization. The same distrust penetrates both management and union groups, pitting managers against other managers and union members against other union members. There is also distrust based on age, sex, race, seniority, work ethics, and work groups who were integrated from merged companies. This situation does not encourage a responsible work environment where common performance goals must be achieved as a team.

"I must admit that trying to change the behavior of both management and the union labor workforce from adversarial behavior to a supportive team environment is a difficult task to achieve. However, after hearing about the CABLE rewiring makeover, I now have a glimmer of hope."

It was getting late and everyone began saying goodbye until next Monday's gathering. They left the meeting wondering how Donna was going to deal with her doubts about her own responsible behavior. Would she be influenced by the team members playing the blame game? Only Joe knew the answer to that question.

CHAPTER NINE

Connecting the Dots Between Donna's Past and Current Behaviors.

WHEN JOE ARRIVED AT THE COFFEE SHOP FOR THE NEXT GATHERING, HE again noticed younger patrons among the crowd. He smiled, welcomed them to the group, and surveyed the crowd to sense the level of interest.

When everyone was settled, Joe wasted no time continuing Donna's story. "At last week's meeting, I ended the story with Donna searching for answers to explain why she always behaved responsibly at her job," he said. "At a previous gathering, I covered Robert's workplace story. In Robert's case, he behaved irresponsibly. His irresponsible behavior was driven at first by his unconscious need to be liked by his subordinates, and later, by his panic to change his management style in seeking a promotion.

"Irresponsible and responsible behaviors are not inborn traits. Both types of behavior are learned when people are stimulated to respond to situations in their environment. When people respond to stimuli, they absorb and filter what they observe from their own unique perspectives. Their actions toward their jobs, other people, and activities are influenced by their work culture, attitudes, emotions, values, and so forth. Based on the consequences of their responses, the outcome of experiencing pleasure or pain determines if a person will repeat his or her actions.

"For example, when Donna was a toddler, she came upon her mother's sewing kit. The red, tomato-shaped pincushion caught her eye, and in moments, she had stuck her finger with a sharp little pin. Her mother cleaned the pinprick and put a pink Band-Aid on the tiny wound, but Donna didn't touch a pincushion again until she was old enough to know how to handle needles and pins safely. Even then, she was always overly careful when sewing. The consequence of experiencing the pain wired the nerve pathways in her brain, teaching her to avoid touching sharp objects. She may not have remembered of the pain of that early moment, but her unconscious mind stored it away as permanent knowledge.

"Donna's behavior in this example is shared by all people. Her behavior was driven by the need to seek pleasure and avoid pain. Her behavior was wired by learning from the consequences of her actions. If she experienced pain from the outcome of an action, she would most likely avoid repeating that behavior. In contrast, if she experienced pleasure from the outcome of an action, she was likely to repeat her behavior. Her learned behavior became part of her behavioral makeup that could have a ripple effect in influencing others.

"Donna was now trying to get in touch with her past and unconscious mind in order to shed some light on why she behaved responsibly in the workplace environment in responding to most situations, even when it was not to her advantage to do so. Donna was frustrated with the way her team played the blame game after missing a deadline for a project. The missed deadline proved to be costly to the company in lost opportunity for sales.

"When Donna needed to relieve stress from work, she followed the routine of going to a local gym for a physical workout and then talking to her friends. Exercise, weight control, proper nutrition, a good support system, and keeping a positive outlook on life was her way of being responsible for her health and well-being. So she left her office and headed to the gym for her daily physical workout.

"As Donna went through her warm-up stretches, her mind slipped back into the past. After she finished warming up, she got on the treadmill and started jogging. While she jogged, her thoughts continued to travel farther back into her past, searching for answers that would help her make a behavioral connection. Her wandering mind first recalled an event that left an indelible impression on her life. It happened back in the sixth grade when she took a math test. She thought over the details of the event until it seemed to have happened only yesterday.

"She remembered the event this way: One day Donna entered her sixth grade classroom, and smiled at her teacher, Mrs. Parker. Donna was feeling confident and ready for a math test. She had studied hard and gotten perfect grades on Mrs. Parker's tests thus far.

"As Mrs. Parker passed out the questions, she said, 'Look around the room and you may find some changes that will help you with the test. But, remember that anyone caught cheating will receive an automatic F on this test.'

"The answers came easily to Donna and she sailed through the questions. All but one, that is, which gave her a bit of trouble. Stumped, she thought for a few moments and then remembered Mrs. Parker's hint. *'Hmm,'* Donna thought, *'Look around the room.'* As she did, her sharp mind caught the clue. *'Oh! The desks are set in a square! That's the answer!'* At that same moment, Donna's eyes accidentally swept across the paper of Kenny, the very smart boy who sat next to her, and she saw that he had come to the same conclusion. Donna felt queasiness in her stomach. As she looked at Kenny's paper, she wrote 'square' in the blank and handed in her paper.

"The following day when the tests were returned, Donna saw that she had received another perfect score. Walking home that afternoon, she thought about what had happened. The comforting sight of her mother opening the door and greeting her burst the dam of the young girl's emotions and she dissolved into tears.

"'Oh, baby,' her mother said, gathering up her daughter in a hug 'What's the matter? Are you okay?'

"'Mommy, I think I did something really bad in school yesterday,' Donna sputtered through her tears, 'You are not going to be proud of me.'

"Donna told her tale as her mother led her to the couch. They sat down next to each other. 'Even though I found the clue and got the answer, seeing that Kenny got it, too, made me certain I was right. I looked at his paper, Mom! I deserve an F. What should I do?' She began to cry once more.

"'Well, honey, if I understand your story, you came up with the answer on your own before you saw Kenny's paper. I do not consider that cheating. After all, the teacher had given everyone advice to look around to find the clue to the answer. But you should do what you think is right,' her mother responded.

"'I want you to know I *am* proud of you for being so honest. Being truthful will earn you self-respect and the trust of others in life. I'm glad you shared this with me, and it pleases me to know that you have such a strong conscience.'"

Joe added, "Sixth grade may be the threshold of middle school, but sometimes, when you're eleven years old, a little comfort and a few encouraging words from Mom go a long way.

"The next day, Donna stayed in her seat after the other students had left for the day. She walked slowly over to Mrs. Parker and told her what had transpired during the math test.

"'So, I really didn't deserve the 100 percent I got. I know the rule: cheating gets you an F.' She had to press her lips together very tightly to keep the tears at bay.

"Mrs. Parker considered the situation for a moment and said, 'Thank you for your honesty, dear. Your grade stands. You came up with the answer yourself and only used Kenny's answer for confirmation. While not a good thing to do, it is not truly cheating.' Donna looked up in surprise and gratitude. 'Thank you, Mrs. Parker!' the girl squealed. Any doubts that may have crossed Donna's mind whether she had done the right thing in being honest were expelled from her mind.

"A few weeks later Donna's mother met with Mrs. Parker for their parent-teacher conference. 'I have to tell you,' Mrs. Parker said, 'that in my 24 years of teaching, I have never had a student come forward and so honestly accept responsibility for her behavior. Whatever you're doing, keep it up, because you're raising a daughter who will always bring you pride.'"

Joe then paused and posed a query to the listeners. "I want to ask you all, what are your observations of Donna's behavior regarding the math test?"

A teenaged girl raised her hand.

"Yes," Joe said. "Please tell us what you think."

"Donna didn't cheat on purpose," the girl said, "but in her heart she knew seeing Kenny's answer made her feel better about her own. Even though she was scared of getting an F, she had the courage to tell the teacher anyway. That's really brave. I don't know if I would have the guts to do it. I have respect for her strong character, and I wish everyone would act like that. It would result in a better world."

"Well," Joe said, "the whole point of honesty is asking yourself who the first person is that you have to be honest with."

"Yourself?" the girl ventured.

"Right!" Joe said.

"There are three principles of responsible behavior that Donna applied in responding to the situation that occurred during the math test," Joe commented.

Before Joe could mention them, Barbara interrupted the discussion and said, "Let me guess. These three principles were:

1. **Be honest with yourself and others in both words and actions.**

2. **Admit your mistake; it is better to lose face than try to save face on false pretenses.**

3. **Have the courage to do the right thing when confronted with a difficult situation that challenges your strength of character.**"

"You got them all, Barbara, thanks!" Joe said. "These principles should be used to help guide people in the workplace and in their everyday lives. When Donna applied these principles, there were lessons learned and benefits gained."

"Yes," said Ellen, "I think I can list those lessons and benefits." Ellen was not used to speaking in front of this many people and she felt a little self-conscious. Susan, who was sitting next to her, nudged her with her elbow. As Ellen hesitated before sharing her insights, she turned to see Susan smiling and nodding at her. The encouragement was enough for Ellen to go on.

"Okay," Ellen began, "the lessons learned and benefits Donna experienced are as follows:

1. Donna learned that being honest earned respect and the trust of others.

2. Admitting your errors builds others' confidence in you.

3. Being courageous earned her the reputation of bravery, justice, and fairness."

"Exactly! Thank you Ellen," Joe said.

Joe picked up on how quickly and intensely the coffee shop patrons were responding to the story. He didn't know if their quick response was due to the caffeine in their drinks, or if the crowd was just excited to hear about ordinary people who are capable of responsible acts in today's environment. In previous discussions, the coffee shop group had acknowledged that they only had to turn on the daily news these days to hear about irresponsible acts, like the use and sale of illegal drugs, acts of violence, sex scandals, political corruption, and so on.

Furthermore, Joe had gleaned that many people had been turned off by the disproportionate time the media spends covering the irresponsible acts of celebrities. Regardless, Joe was pleased by the intense engagement in the story. He looked at his watch and noticed that it was time to end the discussion. They had been going over their agreed-upon hour almost every week, and the enthusiasm about being responsible he sensed in the group influenced his own behavior. He had to smile to himself as he began to wrap up the meeting.

"In summary," Joe began, "Being responsible for your actions begins with being honest with yourself. Face the music and you will feel better about yourself, whatever the outcome. This act of responsibility may require the courage that Donna demonstrated.

"Now, I would like all of you to go home and think about that. Moreover, I suggest that you consciously practice being honest with yourself at least once in the upcoming week. Next Monday I hope you will all come back to hear about an event that took even more courage than Donna's response to her childhood math test."

CHAPTER TEN

To Tell or Not To Tell

THE WEEK WENT BY QUICKLY, AND SOON MONDAY ARRIVED AGAIN. JOE looked around the coffee shop and smiled and said, "Thanks for coming. Your interest in my ideas is very gratifying and I want you to know how much I appreciate your presence and your input. Of course, I hope what I'm telling you will help you in your desire to act responsibly and be role models for others. And I also want you to know that every week, I learn things from your input that solidifies and enhances my theories."

"You go, Joe," Brian said, and a spontaneous round of applause showed Joe that his audience was happy to be acknowledged. "Thanks," he said, and realized he was deeply moved by this group of people giving their time and energy to these meetings. He took a sip of his coffee to give himself a moment to feel his emotions and then began his talk.

"I want to describe for you how Donna continued to access her unconscious mind for events from her past that would help validate her current responsible behavioral pattern in the workplace. Here's a brief summary for the newcomers: Donna was having doubts about always responding responsibly to situations in the workplace.

108

She was seeing that her team members and co-workers were beginning to take advantage of her.

"She hoped that thinking about her past would help her understand why she was so committed to taking responsibility to such an extreme that it sometimes amounted to playing the blame game herself—only she always blamed herself and let others do the same. We left Donna in the gym last week—her safe haven for releasing stress by thinking through events that troubled her.

"Donna completed her jogging exercise on the treadmill. She was drenched with sweat, her muscles tense, but her nerves were beginning to relax. After she recalled her sixth grade math test and the events that followed, she felt good about the outcome. Her confidence was restored and she started her workout on the exercise bike. But her mind continued to drift into the past. This time she recalled an incident that took place when she was in high school.

"One day, Donna walked into her school's computer room and noticed a student named Eric working on one of the computers. Eric was a straight A student, and rumor had it that he liked Donna. She noticed that there was an operating system program on the computer screen. Eric was inputting different codes as if trying to access a database.

"'Hey, Donna, what's up? I'm just working on that essay for English.'

"'Hi, Eric,' Donna replied. 'Are you writing an essay about computer codes? It would be pretty interesting to hear that read in class.' Being a very courteous person, this was as close as Donna could get to telling Eric she didn't think it looked like he was working on an essay.

"Eric quickly minimized the screen. Donna could see the word processing program had been running behind it, and that there was indeed an essay on the screen.

"Donna didn't give this too much thought, until the next day when she saw Eric and another student named James in the computer room again, and this time they were clearly working on entering different codes into an operating system.

"'What are you guys working on?'

"'Nothing much, just playing video games and writing essays. Oh, and trying to crack into the school database for kicks. It's actually a bit of a challenge,' Eric said with a disarming grin.

"Both Eric and James were known as computer whiz kids who had a reputation in their school for being boastful about their ability to crack computer security walls. They were considered 'white hat hackers' who liked to crack computers just for the challenge and bragging rights. It was not their intent to crack computer security walls for malicious advantage. They wanted to use their computer expertise for a career later in life and felt their actions simply sharpened their skills.

"Although they were both top students, their smarts weren't always matched by responsible behavior outside the classroom. Their fellow students often described the pair as self-centered, mischievous, and, by the envious, as adventurous. They seldom took responsibility for their actions, and seldom considered the consequences before acting. They seemed to believe they were smart enough to get away with anything they felt like doing.

"'It might be a challenge, but it's not such a good idea, y'know,' Donna said hesitantly. 'Computer hacking is illegal.' This time Donna was unmoved by Eric's smile.

"'I bet if I could learn how to get past security walls, I could get a job with a computer company to design protection against computer hacking,' Eric said.

"'What about breaking the law?' Donna countered incredulously. 'If you get caught and have that on your record, you might have trouble getting any job, no matter how much you know. So why ruin your chances just for a thrill?'

"'Some computer hackers have never been caught. No one will ever know who did it.'

"'That's impossible,' Donna said. 'If you succeed in breaking into the school records, *you'll* know, and then that knowledge becomes a part of your conscience that you'll have to live with for the rest of your lives.'

110

"The other student, James, finally spoke up and said, 'Donna, where is your sense of adventure and challenge in life? Heck, where's your sense of humor?'

"'My idea of adventure is to take a trip to Africa, and my challenge would be to discover a cure for AIDS, Alzheimer's, cancer, or diabetes.'

"'Well, that might be challenging, but it doesn't sound like much fun,' Eric said. 'You're such a goody-two-shoes, Donna! Lighten up!'

"'Whatever,' Donna said. She went to class, leaving the boys in the computer room. What Eric had said had hurt her. She felt very 'un-cool'. However, she felt even worse about what the two boys were doing. The whole thing left her upset and anxious.

"The next day in math class it was rumored that someone had erased all the grades in the, database. An investigation was in process to identify the culprits. Donna felt very uncomfortable, because she knew immediately that Eric and James must have done it. She was sure she'd never been in such an awkward position before.

"She knew she should let an adult know, but if she did, the label 'tattle-tale' would be added to 'goody-two-shoes.' There were other options Donna mulled over in her mind on how she could handle this situation.

She thought to herself, *'I could confront Eric and James. But, their attitudes when I tried to reach them in the computer room tell me they might just laugh in my face and call me more names. Or, I could tell someone else, but that would only spread the rumor and I didn't actually witness them cracking the database. Or, I could say nothing and hope Eric likes me more for doing that. And then, if I told on them, what are my friends going to think of me? That could be a major social disaster for me!'*

"She desperately wanted to be accepted by her peers, but after mulling over her options, she knew it would be the right thing to tell someone. Getting caught might stop the boys from going any further with their dishonest behavior.

"After school, Donna told her parents what had happened. She also admitted to them that she found Eric attractive.

"Donna's parents felt that their daughter would do the right thing and didn't try to fix the situation for her. However, her parents were surprised to hear that Donna had some feelings toward Eric, which made her decision even harder. It was the first time that Donna had shared information about a boy she liked. Donna's mother sensed her daughter's dilemma and gave her a big hug of support.

"Both of Donna's parents offered guidance in her decision making processes, and praised her openness and honesty in discussing it with them. 'Listen, sweetie,' her father said, 'I have some guiding principles I use in making decisions. I think sharing them with you right now might help you deal with this situation.'

"'Please, Dad, I'd really like to know them!' Donna replied.

"'I'd be happy to,' her father said. 'First,' he began, 'in a difficult situation, I try being honest with myself and the others involved. Second, I pull up the courage to do the right thing, especially in stressful situations that challenge my strength of character. Third, whatever I decide to do, I know I need to take full responsibility for my decision.'

"Donna had listened carefully to her father, and she thanked him for his support and wisdom.

"The next day at school, Donna went to the office to talk with Mr. Walker, the school counselor and Vice Principal. Donna made it clear that she hadn't seen the boys get into the database. Mr. Walker thanked Donna for sharing this information and said he would follow up with an investigation.

"Donna left the meeting with mixed emotions. On the one hand, she liked Eric. On the other, she thought he was wasting his intelligence that could surely be put to better use. She also realized that any friendship they might have had was probably ruined now.

"Eric and James were expelled three weeks after they hacked into the school computer database and erased the grades, but the school decided not to file a complaint, which could have resulted in criminal charges. The boys would have to find new schools to attend, but at least they wouldn't have police records.

"Donna hoped that Eric and James could start over at another school and learn from the consequences of their actions. She was sad that she would never see Eric again, but deep within herself she knew, without any doubt, that she had done the right thing. Instead of earning the reputation of a tattletale, she gained a reputation of respect and admiration for what she had done."

Joe paused and spoke to the group. "I'd like you to think about Donna's situation," he said. "She was caught between a rock and a hard place. What do you think about what she did? Would you have done the same?"

A newcomer, a man in his forties, stood up to speak. "She didn't give in to peer pressure," he said. "She didn't let her emotions cloud her judgment. I'm a teacher, and I can't think of any kids who would be that responsible in this day and age of school shootings, gangs, and drugs." He sat down to a brief smattering of applause.

"What is the responsible behavior principle applied to what Donna did? What are the benefits gained in this situation?" Joe asked.

A young woman Joe had seen at a few of the meetings but who had not spoken before, raised her hand and spoke with reluctance and skepticism. "Hi, I'm Maria" she said, "I've seen people respond in a lot of different ways to situations like Donna's and I kind of agree with what the last person said—it's difficult to believe that people today—kids or adults—would be as selfless and responsible as Donna ended up being. But I think I get your point, Joe, and I think this stuff is really important. So, well, I'm going to give this a shot.

"The responsible behavior principle in play here," Maria offered, "is having the courage to do the right thing when confronted with an ordeal that challenges your strength of character. Donna liked her friend Eric, but didn't let her feelings toward him compromise her judgment in doing the right thing.

"The benefit Donna gained from being courageous in the computer hacker situation," she continued, "earned her the reputation of bravery, justice, and fairness. Is that what you're looking for?"

"Thanks, Maria, that was very well put," Joe responded. "I appreciate you sharing that with us. Your doubts are very understandable, given that in today's society, maintaining good character requires hard work controlling emotions, impulses, actions, and words. It's true that good character in kids today isn't seen as often as we'd hope. Maybe, if we all start focusing on responsible behavior and start seeing more of it in the mirror, our kids will see it too. Next week, I'll tell you what happens when Donna has to help students who have given in to peer pressure to drink and drive."

CHAPTER ELEVEN

Un-Designated Driver

WHEN JOE ARRIVED AT THE COFFEE SHOP, HE PICKED UP WHERE HE HAD stopped last week. As usual, he summarized the story to update the newcomers, and then continued telling Donna's tale.

"Coming out of her reverie, Donna stopped pedaling on the exercise bike. Again, she was drenched with sweat, but her muscles soon began to relax and her nerves settled down. Thinking about her past, and recalling how she handled the incident about Eric and James, left her feeling good. She had a sense of pride about the outcome. However, her reminiscence did not completely clear up the doubts she was experiencing in the present. When she started her workout on the stair climber her mind drifted again to the past. This time she recalled an incident that took place during her senior year in college.

"Donna entered a college that had a good program for her chosen field, but it was also known as a 'party school,' where students stayed up late partying and often skipped classes. There had been several sexual assaults on campus, and drug and alcohol use were common in some areas. Donna's parents had given her strong values to draw upon when responding to the college's behavioral environment. They had cautioned her to be careful moving around campus, and like most parents, they worried about Donna's safety and called her frequently.

"Donna missed her family, and was glad she had the sort of parents who kept in close touch, but she was also excited about college life. Her self-esteem and confidence were high. She had developed a strong sense of self, and had the perseverance to pursue worthy goals with patience and determination. She had high ambitions, and wanted to go into textile chemistry research. She mixed well with other students, and making new friends now seemed effortless for her.

"While Donna's parents often openly discussed the dangers of using drugs and alcohol, a social situation that happened in Donna's senior year severely tested her strength of character.

"A small group of students wanted to go out to a neighborhood restaurant and bar. Donna agreed to go with three of her friends, Alice, Claire, and Melanie. They were celebrating Claire's 21st birthday. Donna's car was in the shop, so Melanie drove to the restaurant. It was Saturday and the place was packed with college students. There was also a big crowd of students in the parking lot openly drinking beer and smoking marijuana.

"Donna's friends ordered a pitcher of beer. Donna didn't usually drink alcohol, and decided not to that evening. As the partying went on, Donna grew concerned with Melanie's ability to drive. Melanie just laughed and said, 'But Donna, I know you'll drive us home. You're the sober one.'

"'But what if I weren't?' Donna asked. 'You assumed I would be sober, and I am, but what if I wanted to party, too?'

"Melanie pretended to be shocked. 'Donna, you never party,' she said. 'We know we can cut loose if you're around to make sure everyone gets home okay.'

"'Is that why you invited me?' Donna asked.

"'Not just for that,' Melanie said. 'You're not that nerdy for a straight-edge girl.'

"'I'm not straight-edge,' Donna said, trying not to sound defensive. 'I'm just . . . me.' She was taken aback that her friends would classify her as 'nerdy' based on the fact that she was smart and responsible.

"Why were positive qualities, like being smart and taking responsibility, looked down upon?" Joe asked. "Donna felt isolated, and though she knew such thinking was common on campus, she would never understand this seeming contradiction. Luckily, her parents' consistent behavior and influence had given her a solid sense of self. She didn't cave in just to be liked, although she felt put out that her friends assumed she would drive them home. She wondered if she were being used. Over the course of her college career, Donna found herself feeling this way from time to time, usually when a friend acted irresponsibly and assumed that Donna would take responsibility.

"Donna's thoughts returned from her past to face the reality of her current situation at work. As she slowed her pace to a cool down mode on the stair climber, she became aware of a connection between the way she had felt used by her college friends and the way she felt she was currently being used by her staff and co-workers.

"Although her feelings of being used may have crossed her mind briefly during past incidents, and raised some occasional doubts about her own behavior, it was never enough to cause concern. The doubts she felt in the present were much stronger than in the past. She wondered what the driving force behind her feelings, thoughts, and actions was. She wanted to make sense of her behavior, and came to the realization that she must find answers in order to move forward with her life. *These doubts are beginning to gnaw at my conscience,'* she thought to herself. Donna finished her workout with uncertainty about how the human behavioral system works. She was still seeking validation for her doubts regarding her responsible behavior."

Joe paused. "Okay, everyone. What do you think Donna should do?" There was a short silence followed by a murmuring. As people began raising their hands, Joe noticed that there wasn't enough time for a deep discussion.

"Let's take some time to think it over," Joe said. "Come back next week to hear what the Magical Mirror has to say to Donna."

CHAPTER TWELVE

Donna Takes a Good Look at Herself

A T THE NEXT MEETING, JOE CONTINUED THE STORY. "DONNA RECALLED HER mother telling her that when searching for answers to problems in your life, you should look deep within yourself, and then have a face-to-face talk with the person you see in the mirror. Donna's mother had faith that the person Donna saw in the mirror would do the right thing.

"As Donna prepared for bed, she stood in front of the mirror thinking about her mother's advice. She looked at her face, noticing a strong nose like her father's, and shimmering eyes like her mother's. Suddenly her reflection blurred and contorted into strange angles; Donna became worried that something was wrong with her vision. Then, a calm voice spoke in hushed tones.

"'Who do you see in the mirror?' the voice asked. Although stunned by this, Donna felt a comfortable presence emanating from the voice. It was warm and soothing, and seemed to want to help her. She felt herself slipping into a trance-like state.

"'I see an over-responsible person who keeps getting taken advantage of,' Donna said.

"'It sounds like you could use a behavior makeover,' the Magical Mirror said.

"'You mean like on TV, where they change your appearance and make you beautiful?'

"'Well, not exactly, but you will be a beautiful person from a holistic perspective when you finish the makeover. The kind of makeover I'm talking about involves an innovative, holistic rewiring of the HUMAN CABLE SYSTEM,' the Mirror explained.

"'I've never heard of the HUMAN CABLE SYSTEM. What's that?' Donna asked.

"'It's a system of nerve pathways conditioned by pleasurable and painful experiences,' the Mirror said. 'The HUMAN CABLE SYSTEM is your thinking. It involves the types of consequences, feelings, actions, learning, and environments you have experienced. I'm going to show you a story to help you better understand.'

"As Donna gazed into the mirror, a scene unfolded before her eyes as though she were watching a movie. She saw a room and six people seated around a conference table—a man who appeared to be the leader, and five other people. Each of the five people wore a white T-shirt that had a letter on it: **C**, **A**, **B**, **L**, and **E**.

"The man began to speak, 'I am Mr. Smith, the training facilitator.' he said. 'You are here from your various business, government, and school organizations to develop team skills and team identity. First, you must focus on getting to know each other so you can develop a shared vision, mission, and a name for the team. However, before the group begins its first task for the session, let's go around the room and introduce ourselves and your goal for attending the team skills session.'

"The participants looked around the room to see who would be the first to speak up. Then, the woman with '**C**' on her shirt spoke up.

"'My name is Consequence, and I'm attending this session to help people be accountable for the outcomes of their actions.'

"'My name is Attitude,' the man with an '**A**' on his shirt announced. 'My goal is to help people maintain a positive feeling as opposed to a negative one toward situations in their lives.'

"The man with 'B' on the front of his shirt was the next to reply. 'My name is Behavior,' he said. 'My goal for attending the team-building session is to help people act more responsibly.'

"The man with an 'L' on his shirt introduced himself. 'My name is Learning,' he said. 'I am attending this training session to help people understand how all the other elements of human behavior work together. Especially,' he emphasized, 'to help people learn from the consequences of their actions, so they can avoid making the same mistakes in the future.'

"The last person, the woman with an 'E' on her shirt, said, 'My name is Environment, and I represent the behavioral environment created by people, as opposed to Mother Nature or the creation of a higher power,' she said. 'I am here to help people create and maintain a positive atmosphere as a model in today's society.'

"'Thank you,' Mr. Smith said. 'For your first team task, you are to develop a name, mission, and vision, but not necessarily in that order, for your team. The name must combine each individual role into one common role for the team, and reflect what the team needs to do to accomplish its purpose and realize its goals. Let's start with a mission statement that everyone can embrace. Would anyone like to draft a mission statement for the group?'

"'Yes,' said L, 'how about this?' He stood and went to the white board at the front of the room and wrote:

> **Team's Mission:** To ensure that people have an Attitude of positive feelings, make responsible actions their main Behavior, seek favorable outcomes as the Consequences of their Behavior, increase their understanding by Learning, and function in an Environment with a positive behavioral atmosphere when responding to situations at work and in their daily lives.

"The other team members nodded their heads in agreement, and A said, 'That sums up each of our different roles in providing services to change people's behavior.'

"'Good!' Mr. Smith said. 'Our next task is to develop a vision statement for the team. To do this, imagine how good at your specialty you want to be, and what level of excellence you want to achieve when carrying out your mission. Who wants to offer a suggestion for a vision statement?'

"'I will try to verbalize a vision for the team,' Learning said.' How about something like this? Become a global provider of a common sense human behavioral process that is designed to improve the workplace behavioral environment, and assist people in life to enhance productivity and to promote a responsible behavioral society.'

"'Does anyone have anything to say about this suggestion?' Mr. Smith asked the team.

"'I would like to add *morale* to productivity,' B said. The other team members nodded their heads in agreement and Mr. Smith wrote the team's vision on the board.

Team's Vision: Become a global provider of a common sense human behavioral process that is designed to improve the workplace environment, and assist people in life to enhance productivity and morale, and promote a responsible behavioral society.

"'Let's take a 15-minute break before we try to come up with a name for the team,' Mr. Smith said. After the break, all the team members had returned to the training room except Behavior. They waited for a few more minutes until Behavior walked in.

"'Sorry for being late, but I received a phone call from the TV cable repair guy. The cable has gone out on me again, and the repairman said that I either needed a new cable or he has to rewire the old one, which could cost as much as getting a new cable.'

"Mr. Smith looked at the five trainees seated in the order of C, A, L, E, and B. Suddenly, he made a connection.

"'Behavior, would you please move your chair between Attitude and Learning?'

"'Uh, sure,' Behavior said. The others made room for him.

"Mr. Smith grinned. 'What do the letters spell?'

"They all looked down at their shirts, and the realization dawned.

"'Well, what do you know,' Learning said. 'I guess we have a name for our team! We're the HUMAN CABLE SYSTEM, aren't we?'

"'Indeed you are,' Mr. Smith acknowledged, and the others smiled and nodded in agreement.

"'Behavior, it was just luck that your cable company called—that's lower case cable, not like *you*—because that gave me an idea,' Mr.

Smith said. 'Just like a TV cable provides clarity in receiving the broadcast signals, so can the HUMAN CABLE SYSTEM provide clarity in receiving signals from the behavioral environments around us. And just as the wires in a TV cable work together, so do the individual wires of the HUMAN CABLE SYSTEM. Together, they create a holistic system—and that is what you are.'

"'I see what you mean,' Learning said. 'For example, in a workplace setting, if the business Environment wiring is a positive one, this creates positive employee Attitude wiring. In turn, that causes positive worker Behavior wiring. Positive Behavior wiring naturally leads to positive Consequences wiring.'

"'Each wire is dependent on the function of the other wires in order to effectively improve and sustain behavior,' Environment added. 'Improving just one or two of the human CABLE wires will only result in short-term gains.'

"'The best way to help improve people's behavior is to give them a human behavior makeover by rewiring a person's CABLE system,' Attitude suggested. 'The way to do that is to teach all people in the world about the five elements of the HUMAN CABLE SYSTEM—or HCS for short—how they interact, and what they can do to help change a person's irresponsible behavior. The decision to change is up to the person, but using the HCS as a tool will help shift society toward a responsible environment.'

"Mr. Smith asked for suggestions from the group for revising the vision, and eventually, they all agreed on a statement. Mr. Smith wrote the revised vision on the board:

> Become a world provider of the HUMAN CABLE SYSTEM™ (HCS) rewiring services that are designed to improve the workplace, and assist people enhance productivity and morale, and promote a responsible behavioral society.

"The mirror concluded that creating a mindset where people look at all of the behavioral elements from an inclusive point of view will result in a sustainable change in behavior.

"As the vision in the mirror faded, Donna saw her own reflection again and took a shocked step backward. She liked the idea of the

Human CABLE System, but wasn't sure how it differed from other behavior modification techniques. Nevertheless, she was willing to learn. The next day, she went off to work mulling this new information over in her mind."

Joe and his audience had been transported from the coffee shop into Donna's story. A cell phone rang in the back of the room and almost in unison, the people in the room blinked and snapped back into the moment. "Sorry!" said the person whose phone had rung, as many heads turned in her direction.

"No problem," assured Joe. "Your phone rang at just the right moment, like a bell telling us it's time to stop for now. I'm sorry we don't have time for a discussion tonight, but come back next week and I'll tell you what happens with Donna's behavioral wiring. Have a great night, and I'll see you next Monday!"

CHAPTER THIRTEEN

Donna's Cable Wiring

THE FOLLOWING WEEK, THE GROUP SETTLED DOWN QUICKLY, ANXIOUS FOR Joe to continue his story. "I can see you are ready to follow Donna on her journey to improving her life—I won't make you wait another minute," Joe said, and got right to it. "After work, Donna was eager to find out if the Mirror would come alive again. When it did, she quickly asked, 'How is the application of the HUMAN CABLE SYSTEM different from how people in today's work environments approach behavior modification?'

"'Good question,' responded the Magical Mirror. 'The major difference is that the CABLE system approaches the human behavior process from a holistic view that encompasses all five conditioning wirings that are shaped by our past experiences of pleasure and pain, or satisfaction and stress. The weakness in today's behavior modification mentality is that it doesn't take into consideration the fact that Environment, Consequence and Learning may have influenced the Attitude and Behavior wiring of the people in the workforce.'

"'One example of this is when a company addresses the negative Attitude and Behavior of the non-management workforce without addressing the negative Attitude and Behavior of management staff,' Donna said.

"'That's a good example,' the Mirror said, and added, 'Another important reason the human CABLE concept works is that most businesses focus on fixing external systems, when the solutions have more to do with the internal character of the personnel who created the system—what I'd call the living human system. Procedures are non-living steps that cannot be carried out without human application.'

"'In other words,' Donna said, 'don't focus on the problem, but rather focus on the source of the problem.'

"'Right! I think you've got it,' the Magical Mirror said. 'Now, on to Part 2 of the Human Behavior Makeover.'

"The voice in the mirror continued, 'After realizing that your wiring needs to be fixed, the second step is to decide which of the wires of your CABLE need fixing. It's not always clear whether all the wires in your CABLE are in need of repair.

"'For example, let's say you've figured out that you need to rewire your Attitude from negative to positive. Negative experiences when we are young and impressionable can create negative thinking patterns that last until we recognize and change them. Awareness of how the HUMAN CABLE SYSTEM works is the first step toward fixing our problems.

"'One of the most common challenges of adult life comes in the form of fitting into a professional environment. Work is so much more than a job. Even if you perform efficiently, if you have a bad Attitude, negativity can undermine your performance. What should you do if you receive a warning from your supervisor that your negative Attitude toward the job is affecting the quality of your work? What if your negative Attitude leads to getting fired? Sadly, this situation is all too common. However, it can be fixed.

"'To change negative Attitude wiring to positive Attitude wiring, you need to change the Behavior wiring to engage in favorable actions. A favorable action will be followed by the favorable Consequence; in this case higher quality work. The Learning wiring needs to be engaged as well. The Consequence must be internalized, and the favorable Behaviors that led to the positive Consequence must be acknowledged as the correct Behavior. This sequence of events will then carry over to the future.

"'A big part of knowing which wires to fix can be accomplished by making the connection between your current CABLE wiring and your past experiences that were conditioned by pleasure and pain. Knowing where the wiring went wrong can show you how to fix it.

"'Donna, I want you to recall a situation from your past CABLE wiring experience that is similar to your current CABLE experience,' the Magical Mirror instructed. 'I will use the CABLE system thought process to solicit the feelings, actions, consequences, learning, and environment you experienced in that situation. This will help you identify a possible source of your current CABLE profile.'

"Donna recalled the sixth grade math test where she had accidentally seen the answer her classmate had put down. She told the Magical Mirror what had happened.

"'What were your thoughts when you reacted to this situation?' the Mirror asked.

"'Initially, I was confident that I would do well on the test. The instructions from my teacher, Mrs. Parker, were to look for a clue and not to cheat.'

"'What was the outcome?'

"'The 100 percent score I made on the math test was allowed to stand because I was honest with Mrs. Parker,' Donna said.

"'Was the consequence pleasurable or painful?' asked the Mirror.

"'It gave me pleasure when Mrs. Parker let my grade stand.'

"'What was your feeling toward the test before taking it?' asked the Mirror.

"'I felt very sure that I would do well. Being confident gave me pleasure. However, I felt emotional pain because I had done something wrong when I glanced at Kenny's test paper. I could not deny the fact that it made me more confident that my own answer was correct. However, it gave me pleasure knowing that I was honest with my mother, Mrs. Parker, and myself. So, I had mixed feelings about the situation.'

"'What were your actions, meaning Behavior, in this situation?' asked the Mirror.

"'First, I told my mother, and then I told my teacher.'

"'When you took the action to tell your mother and teacher, was it painful or pleasurable?'

"'I was experiencing emotional pain, but I felt it was the right thing to do. I would have had to live with guilt on my conscience if I had lied about the situation. It never occurred to me to not be truthful about what happened.'

"'What did you Learn from the Consequence of this situation?'

"'I learned is that it pays to be honest, and that it requires strength of character to obey your conscience.'

"'Was the Learning experience pleasurable or painful?' asked the Mirror.

"'It was satisfying to know that in today's world, it still pays to be honest. I guess that is a form of pleasure.'

"'What was the behavioral Environment around this situation?' asked the Mirror.

"'The atmosphere was tense,' Donna said. 'After all, it was a test.'

"'How did the surroundings influence your actions?'

"'The competitive atmosphere inspired me to want to do my best.'

"'Was that atmosphere experience pleasant or unpleasant?' asked the Mirror.

"'Pleasant for me, because I thrive on competition,' Donna said.

"'Very good, Donna. You are doing just fine,' said the Mirror. 'You have completed the CABLE system profile of a situation from your past. Take a deep breath, relax, and let's take a five minute break.'

"During the break, Donna's memory of the incident that had happened some sixteen years ago caused her to think about her behavior now. She thought to herself that not much had changed since that incident.

"After the break, the Magical Mirror told Donna they would next work on getting a current Human CABLE System profile for her.

"'What is the most recent situation where you felt your wiring needed to be changed?' the Mirror asked.

"'I am the leader for a research project that did not meet an important target date for a deadline. When I called a meeting with my co-workers to resolve the issue, they began pointing fingers and blaming each other for missing the target date.'

"'What were your thoughts when you reacted to this situation?'

"'My initial reaction toward missing the target date was focused on resolving the issue. My second reaction was to determine what could be learned from that situation to keep it from happening again. My third reaction was to examine my own efforts, because I wondered, as Project Manager, if I could have done more to avoid the problem.'

"'Donna, what was the outcome of your action?'

"'I took full responsibility for missing the target date.'

"'Was the consequence that you experienced from missing the deadline pleasurable or painful?' asked the Mirror.

"'Well, it wasn't pleasurable,' Donna said.

"'What were your feelings toward missing the target date?'

"'I was frustrated and disappointed that we had failed. I was also frustrated with my co-workers.'

"'Were your feelings pleasurable or painful?'

"'It was painful to accept the reality that we missed the deadline, and to see my co-workers playing the blame game and not spending more time on resolution.'

"'What was your Behavior as a result of missing the target date?' asked the Mirror.

"'I acted to clarify that, as Project Manager, I was responsible. I then asked the team to determine what went wrong so we could avoid making similar mistakes in the future.'

"'Were your actions seeking pleasure or avoiding pain?'

"'I took pleasure in knowing that taking responsibility was the right thing to do. Taking responsibility also gave me satisfaction. I knew that I would not have to feel guilty. I knew I had been responsible without blaming others. So in that way, I was also avoiding pain.'

"'What did you Learn from the Consequences of this situation?'

"'I learned that my co-workers would allow me to take the blame.'

"'Was the Learning experience pleasurable or painful?' asked the Mirror.

"'Learning that was painful. It made me worry that I will always be taken advantage of.'

"'What was the behavioral Environment within the meeting with your co-workers?' asked the Mirror.

"'They played the blame game.'

"'How did that Environment influence your actions?'

"'It was frustrating seeing the team members pointing fingers. Their Behavior influenced me to take responsibility for missing the target date. In my way of thinking, nothing is ever resolved or gained by blaming others,' said Donna.

"'Was the surrounding experience pleasant or unpleasant?' asked the mirror.

"'The blame-filled behavior displayed by my co-workers was painful,' said Donna. 'Nothing got resolved. Their lack of responsibility stole away valuable time that was needed to resolve the problem.'

"'Being armed with this information should help you understand why you reacted the way you did,' the Magical Mirror said.' Can you tell me what you learned about the distinction between your past and present CABLE systems?'

"'I can see now that there were three behavior principles that stood out in my past CABLE system wiring,' Donna responded. 'These principles were: Being responsible and accountable for my actions, being honest with myself and others in words and actions, and having the courage to do the right thing and follow my conscience instead of the crowd. My old CABLE was hard wired and conditioned by painful and pleasurable experiences, like the way I reacted to taking the math test in the sixth grade. First, I took responsibility for my Behavior. Then, I chose to be honest, and the Consequence of my action was that Mrs. Parker let my 100 percent grade stand, which gave me pleasure and thus a positive reward.

"'Experiencing pleasure conditioned my Behavior, and that Consequence formed my CABLE wirings. I Learned from the Consequence of my actions that being honest was a responsible Behavior principle to live by.'

"'Exactly,' replied the Mirror.' The CABLE system is based on the understanding that everything people do is shaped by their experience of pain and pleasure, or punishment and reward. When we face situations in our work and in our lives that test our strength of character and the principles that guide us, we define who we are.'

"'What do you think you can do to rewire your CABLE system?' The Mirror asked Donna.

"'I can assertively speak up when I see things going wrong,' Donna answered. 'If one department drops the ball and makes other departments late, I can calmly state what happened without laying blame. I can use a positive Attitude and implement Behavior to come up with solutions to reach a favorable outcome—the desired Consequence—in the future. Approaching the situation in this manner helps rewire the C, A, and B components of my CABLE.

"'Now, I am more aware how all the elements of my CABLE system are dependent on each other to sustain improvement in future behavior. Thus, L and E—the Learning and Environment wiring of my CABLE—must also be included in this situation. I can learn from this experience and maintain a positive atmosphere in resolving future problems.'

"Donna felt relieved. She now understood herself better, and she knew that changing her behavior was a simple matter of rewiring the five elements of her own human behavior process."

Who Do You See in the Mirror?

J OE CONCLUDED HIS STORY, AND THE AUDIENCE APPLAUDED HEARTILY. WHEN they finished, he addressed them once more.

"When you go home tonight, I'd like you all to take the time to take a good look at your wiring," he said. "Think about times when you have behaved in ways that were unproductive, or that you later regretted. Then, like a technician, examine each wire of your CABLE to see where the problem lies. This method is so simple that anyone of any age or ability level can do it. Remember, responsibility starts with the question, 'Who do you see in the mirror?' If you don't like the reflection gazing back at you, then you alone have the absolute ability to change it by rewiring your CABLE." Joe reached into his brief case and brought out a stack of papers. He handed them to Greg and gestured to him to pass the sheets around the room.

"Those of you who have been coming to these gatherings since they began will remember that we created a list of Twelve Common Sense Principles of Responsible Behavior, and the specific benefits of adhering to those principles," Joe said. "Now that you have heard and discussed all the new ideas involved in the CABLE makeover, I believe you are ready to apply them in your lives at work and at home. I leave you with a copy of the twelve principles and their benefits. Those benefits—the Consequences we've been referring to—can be predicted if these principles are adopted to guide you at work and in life.

"I want to thank you for coming to our Monday meetings. I have learned so much from you all, and it is so very gratifying to feel I may have helped you find your true selves in your own Magical Mirrors." What can only be described as a party followed on the spot.

Everyone in the coffee shop, including the servers, joined in a heart-felt toast—with coffee, tea, or hot chocolate standing in for champagne—to the success and satisfaction of the experience they had shared. They all knew their Coffee Shop CABLE workshop would stay with them, and be shared over coffee with others in times to come.

The End of a Beginning—
For a Shift Toward a Society of More Responsible Behavior:
Who Do You See in the Mirror?

The Twelve Principles
of Responsible Behavior

Principle I: Be honest with yourself and others in both words and actions.

Benefits: If a person lives consistently by this principle, they earn the respect and trust of others. Honesty builds self-esteem, character, and confidence. An honest person is considered trustworthy, and able to carry out commitments, obligations, and duties.

Principle II: Be publicly accountable for your own actions and inactions.

Benefits: Trust, confidence, and respect for self and others are earned by being accountable. Being accountable shows true leadership, dependability and reliability. Being accountable displays self-discipline, commitment, pride, and a positive attitude in completing the task.

Principle III: Admit your mistakes. It is better to lose face than to save face on false pretenses.

Benefits: Admitting mistakes is being honest with yourself. Admitting errors builds others' confidence in you.

Principle IV: Have the courage to do the right thing, especially when confronted with a difficult situation that challenges your strength of character.

Benefits: You display bravery, justice, and fairness. You practice unbiased and fair treatment for all human beings regardless of race, gender or economic status.

Principle V: Do not blame others for the consequences of your actions and inactions.

Benefits: Accepting responsibility for your actions and inactions is a sign of genuine leadership. It demonstrates objectivity in resolving issues. You do not become distracted by accusing others.

Principle VI: Be proactive. Consider the consequences of your actions before initiating them.

Benefits: Planning ahead shows rational behavior and can prevent mistakes that you will later regret. It earns you the reputation for making sound judgments instead of being impulsive, emotional, and reactionary.

Principle VII: Do not seek pleasure by inflicting pain on others.

Benefit: Sensitivity and concern for the well being of others are learned behavior, as is selflessness. Demonstrating sensitivity earns the respect of others.

Principle VIII: Take full ownership of your actions.

Benefits: Others will respect you because you are self-confident, a strong leader, and have a strong character. This builds self-worth.

Principle IX: Pursue your own well being while respecting the needs of others and legal rules.

Benefit: You gain a high regard for the well being of yourself, others, and the legal system.

Principle X: Learn from the consequences of your actions and inactions.

Benefit: Being aware of the consequences will help you avoid mistakes in the future.

Principle XI: Be willing to face the consequences of your actions, without letting emotional pain or pleasure compromise the truth.

Benefit: Telling the truth will set you free, regardless of the consequences of your actions.

Principle XII: Be positive in everything you do.

Benefits: Positive attitudes breed positive actions. Positive actions breed positive outcomes. Positive outcomes breed positive learning. Positive learning breeds positive change for future actions that create responsible behavioral environments.

WHO DO YOU SEE IN THE MIRROR?
SELF-IMPROVEMENT WORKBOOK

THE HUMAN CABLE SYSTEM™ (HCS)
A Behavioral Makeover Process

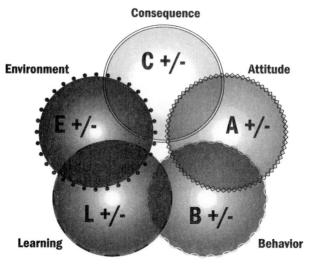

Human CABLE System™ (HCS)

Joseph A. Williams, Ph.D.

Introduction

Everyone in the world—an estimated 6.8 billion of us—exhibits or is influenced by behavior that can be categorized as either irresponsible or responsible actions. Unfortunately, much of the behavior we see in today's society suggests we are shifting toward a culture of irresponsibility. An irresponsible culture is described as being out of control, careless, unwise, immature, and dishonest, corrupt, in a state of denial, and in which people regularly blame others for their own actions.

In contrast, a responsible culture is described as honest with self and others, compassionate, proactive, rational, courageous in doing things right, non-corrupt, respectful of self and others, and in which people publicly take responsibility for their actions. The shift toward irresponsibility is a greater threat to the world's security than nuclear weapons proliferation or guns; the weapons themselves, being non-living objects, do not kill—it's the people's choice to use or launch them into action.

As a solution, the HUMAN CABLE SYSTEM (HCS) is an innovative behavioral makeover process, being presented here for the first time in print. The HCS is built on the premise that global behavioral change can result from individual commitments to practice responsible behavior. The HCS is a simple, common sense approach that has eluded behaviorist gurus for years and is now expected to revolutionize the self-help movement. HCS does not attempt to reinvent the wheel; instead, it repackages existing behavioral knowledge about people's actions and/or inactions into real life situations.

HCS breaks the cycle created when people change their behavior for a short time but later revert back to previous behavior. One common example of rollercoaster behavior is when some people are not able to stay on a healthy diet to control their weight. The HCS process answers the question "why is it so difficult for people to change and maintain responsible behavior when the responsible behavior change will resolve most issues they face in life?" In response to that question, HCS deals directly with the root cause of the erratic highs and lows of behavioral change. HCS offers a simple common sense solution about how to change people's actions and/or inactions to make them responsible and sustainable.

Based on the HCS principles, the *Who Do You See in the Mirror Workbook* provides diagnostic tools to help individuals assess their current behavior status and explore ways to rewire their CABLE toward responsible behavior. Each person can become part of a behavioral environment movement that continuously models responsibility. It starts with a group of one. Eventually the global society shifts, and everyone will have played a part in making the world a better place.

THE HUMAN CABLE SYSTEM™
Behavioral Makeover Process

The HUMAN CABLE SYSTEM is a vehicle for understanding and modifying people's behavior by rewiring the five interactive nerve pathways through the brain. The brain is an organ of the nervous system that is essential for all human functions, including consciousness, memory, thought, behavior, and personality. These pathways are created from conditioned responses to pleasurable and painful situations experienced in the environment. Human survival instinct is driven by the behaviors of seeking satisfaction and avoiding stress that result in the original wiring of the nerve pathways. These pathways are represented by the CABLE acronym: Consequence, Attitude, Behavior, Learning, and Environment. They are defined as follows.

- **Consequence (C +/–)** — an outcome that logically follows an action or inaction. Behavior and consequences have a cause and effect relationship. Consequences are used to predict future behavior.

- **Attitude (A +/–)** — a disposition resulting from learned or inherited tendencies that reflects a favorable or unfavorable state of mind.

- **Behavior (B +/–)** — an action or inaction linked to an environmental response. Driven mainly by attitude, behavior results in a consequence.

- **Learning (L +/–)** — an awareness of the need to gain knowledge or skills in order to change future behavior.

- **Environment (E +/–)** — the surrounding combination of external physical conditions that influences an individual's growth, development, and survival. In this context, environment excludes acts of nature and unexplained phenomena.

Each of these pathways is wired positively or negatively. It is based on how the person reacts to the situation. Positive wiring results in responsible behavior. Negative wiring results in irresponsible behavior. As a functional comparison, just as a TV cable can provide clarity in receiving the broadcast signal, the HCS can provide clarity in receiving the different signals we receive each day from others' actions in the environment around us. And, just as the wires in a TV cable work together, the individual wires of the Human Cable System join to create a holistic system. Using the HCS approach to behavior modification, individuals can rewire their nerve pathways from negative to positive, or the reverse.

To transform irresponsible behavior into responsible behavior, all five CABLE pathways must be wired in a positive way. The rewiring must be approached as an aggregate endeavor, just as the letters in the acronym fit together to spell the word CABLE. Partial rewiring *will not* result in lasting or permanent change. Half-done rewiring has been the mindset for hundreds of years and the result has been an "on again/off again" behavioral pattern. Incomplete rewiring will only result in short-lived behavioral change.

For example, rewiring only (A) and (B) will result in little sustainable behavioral improvement unless (L) and (E) are rewired as well to change the consequence (C). There must be a lesson learned (L) from the results of the consequence (C) to ensure that future behavior is different from that of the initial wiring experience. Thus, C is a key factor in the relationship with A, B, L, and E for the rewiring process. Likewise, rewiring responsible actions must be modeled publicly and continually as part of the global behavioral environment (E) that causes a set of like attitudes (A), which in turn drives behavior (B).

The HCS Model

The model outcome, where all pathways are wired positively, is shown here.

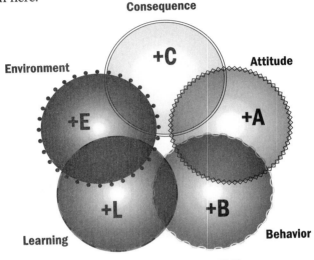

Human CABLE System™ (HCS)

Responsible individuals possess the personality, courage, self-confidence, conviction, willpower, self-control, compassion, and honesty to be accountable for their actions or inaction. In contrast, an irresponsible person does not accept such responsibility—perhaps because of fear, ignorance, denial, selfishness, or choice. These individuals then blame others for the consequences of their behavior, even when there is no question as to where the accountability should lie.

People who desire to rewire their nerve pathways toward more responsible behavior must also be willing to adopt the *Twelve Common Sense Principles of Responsible Behavior* presented here. The twelfth principle, "Be positive in everything you do" is the standard for the HCS process.

The expected results are built on the following premises:
- Positive Attitudes breed positive actions.
- Positive actions (Behavior) breed positive outcomes (Consequence).
- Positive outcomes breed positive Learning.
- Positive Learning breeds positive change for future actions, which in turn creates positive responsible behavioral Environments.

Twelve Common Sense Principles of Responsible Behavior

1. Be honest with yourself and others in both your words and actions.

2. Be publicly accountable for your actions.

3. Admit your mistakes; it is better to lose face than try to save face on false pretenses.

4. Have the courage to do the right thing, especially when confronted with a difficult situation that challenges your strength of character.

5. Do not blame others for the consequences of your actions or inaction.

6. Consider the consequences of your actions before you initiate them.

7. Do not seek pleasure through inflicting pain on others.

8. Take full ownership of your actions.

9. Pursue your own well being while respecting the needs of others.

10. Learn from the consequences of your actions or inactions.

11. Be willing to face the consequences of your actions, without letting emotional pain or pleasure compromise the truth.

12. Be positive in everything you do.

Self-Analysis Questionnaire

Your answers to the following questions will provide you with the necessary feedback to help you begin the behavior makeover process using the HUMAN CABLE SYSTEM. There is no right or wrong response. Answer each question with honesty, using your mirror as a tool for face-to-face self-talk. Circle only one answer per question.

1. How would you describe your behavior when responding to situations in the workplace?

   a. Responsible   b. Irresponsible   c. Both

2. How would you describe your behavior when responding to situations in your personal life?

   a. Responsible   b. Irresponsible   c. Both

3. How satisfied are you with the actions you choose in response to situations in either the workplace or your personal life?

   a. Very satisfied   b. Satisfied   c. Not very satisfied

4. Have you ever tried to change the way you respond to situations?

   a. Yes   b. No

5. Have you ever tried to change irresponsible actions into responsible actions?

   a. Yes   b. No

6. Have you ever acted irresponsibly and then repeated the same behavior?

   a. Yes   b. No

7. How often are you aware of the motivations behind your reactions to situations?

   a. Always   b. Sometimes   c. Never

8. Which of the following statements best describes how you feel about taking responsibility for your behavior, regardless of the consequence?

   a. I always take responsibility for my actions.

   b. I sometimes take responsibility for my actions.

   c. I never take responsibility for my actions.

9. Which of the following statements describes your proactive behavior?

    a. I always consider the consequences of my actions before I act.

    b. I sometimes consider the consequence of my actions before I act.

    c. I never consider the consequence of my actions before I act.

10. Which of the following statements describes how you enhance responsible behavior when you respond to situations in your workplace or personal life?

    a. I always set an example by modeling responsible behavior myself.

    b. I tell others how to model responsible behavior but do not always set an example myself.

    c. I sometimes set an example by modeling responsible behavior.

    d. I never set an example by modeling responsible behavior.

11. How often are you influenced by others people's actions and inactions before deciding to act when responding to a situation?

    a. Always   b. Sometimes   c. Never

12. How often are you aware of how you behave when you react to situations?

    a. Always   b. Sometimes   c. Never

13. Do you see a connection between your present behavior and your behavior during early child development?

    a. Yes   b. No

14. Which of the following words best defines your dominant personality?

    a. Optimist   b. Pessimist   c. Dreamer   d. Realist

15. How would you describe your typical response to situations in your workplace or personal life?

    a. I respond spontaneously without thought.

    b. I respond rationally with thought.

    c. Sometimes I respond both spontaneously and rationally.

Interpreting and Applying Results

The purpose of this self-analysis is to provide you with an awareness of your current behavior. This behavioral analysis is based on the premise that individuals are responsible for their own actions or inaction in response to situations at the workplace and in personal life environments. Regardless of whether you perceive yourself as always, sometimes, or never taking responsibility for your actions, you still have the opportunity to improve and sustain responsible behavior.

For example, a person who *always* takes responsibility for his or her actions is challenged to maintain that status when facing difficult circumstances. On the other hand, a person who is categorized as being responsible *sometimes* for their actions has a greater challenge to improve and maintain consistency. The person who *never* takes responsibility for his or her actions has the greatest challenge to improve behavior.

Nevertheless, all behavioral categories must be addressed directly and effectively, if we are to shift society toward a more responsible environment and make the world a better place to live.

The Human CABLE System

Directions: Think about outstanding situations that occurred during your upbringing. Select one of these situations to use in this exercise. Follow the three steps below to create your behavior profile.

STEP 1: Recall the way you reacted to a situation from your childhood that is similar to the way you reacted to a recent situation. The purpose is to relate the past and present behavior environments. It helps broaden the awareness for future behavior environments.

STEP 2: Use the formatted questions in **STEP 3** to develop a written CABLE profile that reflects past and present experiences. This helps you to connect the similarities and differences between past and current behavior for potential areas to growth.

STEP 3: Develop your HCS written profile by briefly describing the situation to which you reacted. Then answer the following questions to determine the *positive* (+) and *negative* (-) wiring experiences of your CABLE nerve pathways using the self-analysis behavioral profile charts A and B on pages 146 and 147.

Consequence wiring
- What was the outcome of my action in this situation?
- Was the consequence experienced pleasurable (+) or painful (−)?

Attitude wiring
- How did my internal and external environment influence my behavior in this situation?
- Did I experience pleasure (+) or pain (−)?

Behavior wiring
- What were my actions in this situation?
- What were the motivations behind my actions?
- What was I feeling or thinking?
- Was I seeking pleasure (+) or avoiding pain (−) in this experience?

Learning wiring
- What did I learn from the consequence of my actions in this situation?
- Was the learning experience pleasurable (+) or painful (−)?

Environment wiring
- What was the behavioral environment is this situation?
- How did my surroundings influence my actions?
- From what I learned from the consequence of my actions, was the surrounding experience pleasant (+) or unpleasant (−)?

Self-Analysis Behavior Profile Chart (Part A)

Description of Situation:

Consequence Wiring: [___]
Outcome:

Positive or Negative :

Attitude Wiring: [___]
Behavioral Environment Influence factor:

Positive or Negative

Behavior Wiring: [___]
Actions:

Motive:

Feeling or Thinking:

Positive or Negative:

Learning Wiring: [___]
Consequence Learning:

Positive or Negative:

Environment Wiring: [___]
Behavioral Environment:

Surrounding Influence:

Positive or Negative:

Self-Analysis Behavior Profile Chart (Part B)

Assessment Results:

C: Positive _____ or Negative _____

A: Positive _____ or Negative _____

B: Positive _____ or Negative _____

L: Positive _____ or Negative _____

E: Positive _____ or Negative _____

Action Needed for Change:

1.

2.

3.

4.

5.

Follow-Up: 3 months; 6 months; 1 year

The actual assessment results of how all five pathways are wired, is recorded in the chart that follows: These results should be compared with the HCS standard "Be positive in everything you do" principle where five CABLE pathways must be wired in a positive way as an aggregate goal.

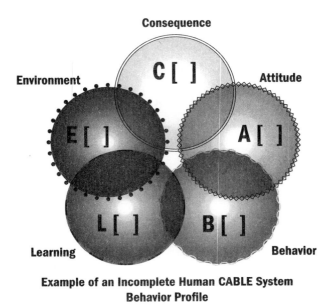

**Example of an Incomplete Human CABLE System
Behavior Profile**

The Situation: Driving Safely on Public Roadways

According to the law enforcement of the state's traffic department, the major cause of automotive accidents that result in death and injures is speeding and driver distraction. Aggressive efforts to share this information with the public have done little to modify driver behavior. However, global change can result from the individual's commitment to responsible behavior.

In this example, the HUMAN CABLE SYSTEM written behavioral profile records how and why the person reacted after exceeding the posted speed limit and being distracted while driving. The driver briefly describes the situation and explains his thoughts, feelings, and actions to create a HCS profile. The self-analysis behavioral profile chart part A and B is presented on pages 149 and 150.

Self-Analysis Behavior Profile Chart (Part A)

Description of Situation: *I exceeded the speed limit, drove on the freeway while talking on the cell phone, and did not leave enough space between my car and the car in front of me. When the car in front of me came to a quick stop, I hit it from behind.*

Consequence Wiring: [–]
Outcome: *In the past, my unsafe driving did not result in an accident. However, this time the outcome was different, and I hit the car in front of me.*
Positive or Negative: *The consequence was painful (negative).*

Attitude Wiring: [–]
Behavioral Environment Influence factor: *My internal behavior was influenced from past experience of exceeding the speeding limit and talking on the phone without resulting in an accident. I was influenced externally by observing that most drivers today drive the same way. My feeling was that accidents happen to others until they happen to you.*
Positive or Negative: *The stress from this experience was negative.*

Behavior Wiring: [–]
Actions: *I exceeded the posted speed limit and talked on the cell phone, thus putting myself and others at risk of serious injuries or death.*
Motive: *My incentive was getting to my destination faster while completing a task on my cell phone. I avoided dealing with my own impatience.*
Feeling or Thinking: *My thought was avoiding being stressed out by traveling at a slower speed and delaying the cell phone task at hand. It did not occur to me that I was just being impatient.*
Positive or Negative: *My actions in this situation resulted in a negative experience.*

Learning Wiring: [–]
Consequence Learning: *I learned my actions were irresponsible. I became conditioned to the experience of seeking my own satisfaction (+) by exceeding the speed limit and talking on the cell phone without regard for the safety of myself and others. Because prior behavior did not result in an accident, I had a false sense of safety. This outcome gave me satisfaction (+) that influenced my decision to continue to behave irresponsibly.*
Positive or Negative: *The awareness of my irresponsible actions resulting in an accident was a negative experience.*

Environment Wiring: [–]
Behavioral Environment: *The behavioral environment of the roadway is characterized by drivers exceeding the posted speed limits and talking on their cell phones.*
Surrounding Influence: *Observing that most of the other drivers were not complying with the posted speed limit and many were talking on the phone had some influence on my decision to do the same.*
Positive or Negative: *Overall, the driving experience was negative.*

Self-Analysis Behavior Profile Chart (Part B)

Assessment Results:

C:	Positive _____	or Negative	__X__
A:	Positive _____	or Negative	__X__
B:	Positive _____	or Negative	__X__
L:	Positive _____	or Negative	__X__
E:	Positive _____	or Negative	__X__

Action Needed for Change:

1. *I need to start with the person I see in the mirror as the sole source of making choices that resulted in the consequence of the car accident.*

2. *I need to modify my driving habits to drive responsibly by rewiring my CABLE from negative to positive*

3. *I need to re-examine some past and present situations that I reacted to, so I can be more consciously aware of how and why my CABLE nerve pathways were initially wired.*

4. *I need to adopt the **Twelve Common Sense Principles Of Responsible Behavior** as part of my daily life practice.*

5. *I need to re-evaluate my CABLE using a follow-up process to determine current status.*

Follow-up: 3 months; 6 months; 1 year

Assessment Results Overview

The Human CABLE System wiring of the driving situation was negative (–). The results of this assessment are depicted below.

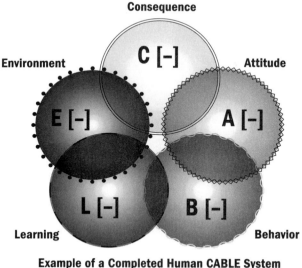

Consequence

C [–]

Environment

Attitude

E [–]

A [–]

L [–]

B [–]

Learning

Behavior

Example of a Completed Human CABLE System Behavior Profile

All five CABLE wiring components need to be rewired to change the behavior to responsible driving habits. Changing only B (–) without modifying the wiring of C (–), A (–), E (–), and L (–) will result in little sustainable improvement in future behavior. The goal is to rewire the negative cable wirings C-, A-, B-, L-, and E-, to positive cable wirings C+, A+, B+, L+, and E+ (i.e., Rewire your HCS to change and sustain future responsible behavior).

This depiction is in direct contrast to the standard where all wiring components should be positive (+) in order to ensure safe road travel. The HCS model is depicted on page 152.

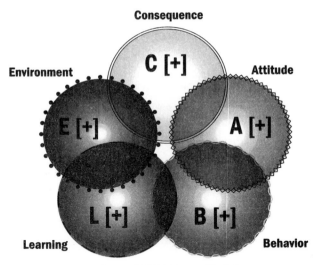

Consequence

Environment

Attitude

C [+]

E [+]

A [+]

L [+]

B [+]

Learning

Behavior

HUMAN **CABLE** SYSTEM **Model**

Summary

The HUMAN CABLE SYSTEM (HCS) behavioral makeover process is a strategy that, while practiced repeatedly on the individual level, has the potential to effect global behavioral change. By wiring five interactive nerve pathways in a positive way, individuals can transform their behavior and contribute to a behavioral environment that models responsibility.

Each of these pathways—Consequence, Attitude, Behavior, Learning, and Environment—must be positively wired as a group to result in lasting change. This rewiring, in combination with adopting the Twelve Common Sense Principles for Responsible Behavior, can shift society toward personal responsibility and make the world a better place to live.